Praise For The Author

This travel guru's story of her adventures in mystical lands is a spell-binding epic that will leave you hankering to follow in her footsteps. Exploring the magical lands of Tibet, Egypt, Peru and more, Sharon interweaves tales of her travels in the world with those of her inner journey of self-discovery - through the secret and subtle world of dreams, symbols and psycho-spiritual phenomena. This book is a breath-taking, vibrant travelogue – and so much more. It's magic. I loved it!!

Linda George,
Astrologer, International Author of Sun Signs and Soul Mates, New Zealand

---

Sharon Breslin's whole life is a continuous journey filled with adventure and genuine spiritual mystery. As an individual she is continuously striving to improve the lives of people she meets in her day-to-day activities. The business side of Sharon is methodical and intuitive. Her Feng Shui Spaces business has enlightened and assisted my media company to grow and think bigger than the formula of strategy. She taught me to feel and combine my inner soul with my analytical mind to achieve the most from my business goals. Her Lifestyle Journeys business promises to take you on your own journey of discovery. There is always something to learn if you open your mind to the opportunities ahead and Sharon has her own special way of delivering this message to all personality types.

Ryan Babbage,
Founder and Strategist of Onstem Media, VIC, Australia and New Zealand

Sharon's harmonious energy, balance and elegance is a gift to us all who strive for peace and success. She shares her knowledge and insight with generosity.

Geraldine Coy,
International Author "Brave Truth"
Leadership and Personal Development

Sharon has an exquisite way of diving into her vast toolbox of gifts to bring out whatever is required for your healing process. Her healing work takes you to the deepest part of yourself, where she effortlessly goes about clearing the cobwebs from your soul. Her keen perception and warmth is very nurturing and she has the most amazing practical insights, which I have used with great success! She has an immense capacity for spiritual and professional guidance.

Olya Bojczuk,
Holistique Hynotherapist, Melbourne, Australia

Spending time with Sharon Breslin is like opening the window in a dark room and allowing the sunlight to brighten your life! Whether you are learning about sacred parts of the world, discovering the mysteries of change and enhancing space through Feng Shui or being a part of an incredible ceremony she is performing, your life is forever changed in a beautiful way! Sharon empowers each person she connects with, in person or through written word and gives them a sense of being sacred, of being whole and celebrating who they are and why they are here on the journey of life.

Luann Cibik,
Master Educator Interior Alignment School of Feng Shui, USA

Sharon Breslin's entrepreneurial spirit is the heart of this book. Her sense of adventure shines and is a witness to her life's purpose which is to lead people. I have travelled many journeys with her to Spain, Sedona and Peru and each has been a unique experience not only because of the knowledge and the professionalism of the tour's guides but the fun, often challenging spiritual dimension each tour encounters. Being a Feng Shui Master Teacher, her ability to spiral the spiritual awareness at visited ancient sites is humbling.

Rosemary Nelson
Feng Shui Practitioner Equate Aligned Environments, New Zealand

---

Sharon is a warm-hearted, open-minded woman who does more than take people on a guided tour – she aims to enhance their spiritual growth with her tours, at the same time as having fun. Indeed, she brings a few skills to the table, being an intuitive healer and a Master Teacher of Interior Alignment – specialised Feng Shui in other words.

Elizabeth Jewell Stephens,
Editor, Living Now, Melbourne, VIC, Australia

MAGICAL TRAVELS

Global Publishing Group
Australia • New Zealand • Singapore • America • London

MAGICAL TRAVELS

A travel guru's guide
to the most mystical and
amazing places
on earth.

Sharon Breslin

DISCLAIMER

All the information, techniques, skills and concepts contained within this publication are of the nature of general comment only and are not in any way recommended as individual advice. The intent is to offer a variety of information to provide a wider range of choices now and in the future, recognising that we all have widely diverse circumstances and viewpoints. Should any reader choose to make use of the information contained herein, this is their decision, and the contributors (and their companies), authors and publishers do not assume any responsibilities whatsoever under any condition or circumstances. It is recommended that the reader obtain their own independent advice.

First Edition 2014

National Library of Australia
Cataloguing-in-Publication entry:

Author: Breslin, Sharon

Title: Magical Travels: A Travel Guru's Guide to the Most Mystical and Amazing Places on Earth / Sharon Breslin.

1st ed.
ISBN: 9781922118394 (paperback)

Voyages and travels
Spirituality
Sacred space
Pilgrims and pilgrimages
Self-analysis (Psychoanalysis)
Self-consciousness (Awareness)

910.4

Published by Global Publishing Group
PO Box 517 Mt Evelyn, Victoria 3796 Australia
Email info@GlobalPublishingGroup.com.au

For further information about orders:
Phone: +61 3 9739 4686 or Fax +61 3 8648 6871

Dedication

I dedicate this book to all the shamans, wisdom keepers and spiritual teachers of this world. Thank you for tirelessly sharing your precious knowledge and gifts. Your selfless commitment to the healing of both the planet and its people is truly appreciated.

To the spirit world, I am forever grateful
for the experiences I have had through my
intuitive healing practice and my travels.
They have expanded my world in ways I
could never have imagined.

Sharon Breslin

Acknowledgements

To have all of the thoughts and experiences that have swirled around in my head for the last 15 years eventually manifest into reality by way of this book is nothing more than a miracle!

Where would you be without those special people in your life? The ones who support you, encourage you and totally believe in you.

It is with much heartfelt gratitude that I would like to take this opportunity to say a huge "THANK YOU" to all of those who played a part in helping me achieve one of my biggest dreams. Please forgive me if I miss anyone.

Willaru Huyatu - Incan Master, one of my greatest teachers. I will never forget the moment you planted the seed, turning to me while travelling together in Peru and telling me I should write a book about my travels. You insisted I was to write journals so that I could refer back to them at a later stage. How right you were, they have been invaluable!

Ricardo Guggenheimer, my Camino tour guide extraordinaire, for your friendship, trust and support. Another amazing teacher.

To Linda George, one of my closest friends, for your unwavering support and guidance. As an accomplished journalist, author, astrologer and let's not forget yoga teacher, you gave your time so generously, encouraging me to write my stories.

Ryan Babbage from Onstem Media for picking me up when the chips were down, believing in me 100% and encouraging me to keep following my dreams. Your guidance, both in business and personal matters, creative skills and loyal friendship is a blessing.

Patricia Treadaway, clairvoyant, for our amazing friendship, your incredibly wise words over the years and your vision in my abilities and what I can achieve, thank you!

Penny Spencer, director of Spencer Travel and one of Australia's top 30 female entrepreneurs, how lucky I have been to meet and work with you since my move to Australia. You are an inspiration and I want to thank you for believing in my ability as a tour operator and Feng Shui practitioner.

To Karen Maurice-O'Leary, creative director, Starseed PR, for choosing to travel with Lifestyle Journeys all those years ago. You have shared your creative ideas time and again helping me far more than you will ever know.

A special thank you to Luann Cibik, my Interior Alignment School of Feng Shui master educator. Your dedication, professionalism wisdom and support has been second to none…they say the teacher appears when the student is ready!

To my dearest friends of whom I have many but there are some who have been behind me the whole way, showing a great depth of interest in my projects. Olya Bojczuk my gorgeous friend from Melbourne, your support has been tireless, thank you! Sylvia Flimm, another amazing astrologer, thank you for all of your encouragement and ever so wise words. Jenny Symmans for your patience and exceptional skill in putting into words what was in my head right at the birthing stage of Lifestyle Journeys Ltd. To the rest of you, you know who you are. You're the best.

To all of my clients who chose Lifestyle Journeys to adventure with, thank you! Without you I would not have had the opportunity to further my travelling and mystical experiences.

Saving the best until last, my beautiful family whom I love dearly, you are my rock in all ways. Dad, for your wisdom and teaching me that I can do anything I set my mind to. Mum, for your belief in me and always being there. Wendy, my accountant, my guru and one of my best friends and Jimmy my loveable rogue of a brother, who has the Irish blarney through and through, for trusting and encouraging me.

To the team at Global Publishing Group, thank you for guiding and supporting me through the process and believing in the book's success.

Sharon Breslin

Author

BONUS

SPECIAL GIFTS

To receive great free bonuses that will complement this book and your own magical travels, head on over to my website

www.lifestylejourneys.com/bonus

Contents

Acknowledgements

Foreword 1

Introduction 3

Chapter 1 – Returning Home 7

Chapter 2 – The Gift of Knowing 29

Chapter 3 – Messages from out of the Blue 45

Chapter 4 – Egyptian Magic 65

Chapter 5 – Navajo Initiation 89

Chapter 6 – Incan Wisdom 121

Chapter 7 – Destiny 155

Author's Final Word 173

About the Author 175

Recommended Resources 179

Foreword

Knowing Sharon is like having light in your life.

I first met Sharon through a client of mine and during our first meeting - a 2 hour lunch - it only took me 5 minutes to know Sharon was not only a special person but we shared one of those wonderfully comfortable connections.

Since that first meeting, Sharon has helped to shape my business through her energy clearing and amazing Feng Shui teachings. There have been many instances where Sharon has come into my businesses and made huge differences, not only spiritually but also with my staff, and allowed opportunities to come forth that may not have come to fruition without her presence. One in particular was a pivotal merger that I really didn't think or see how it could come to actualisation.

Sharon advised me of ways to bring my dream to life with her Feng Shui techniques and unique ability to read the business blueprint and guess what - it worked! I have developed 5 award winning travel companies in Sydney over the past 16 years with over 60 staff. Sharon, having also run award winning businesses, has ensured our friendship and working relationship has remained strong due to having a mutual commonality.

This book is one that will appeal to anyone who loves to travel in any form. I am a five star traveller but can still relate to the self discovery and personal growth that comes with any form of travel. Sharon has interspersed her love of travel with her spiritual journeys and brought us a masterpiece of wonder and enlightenment.

Having just returned from Tibet myself, the true connection you can feel when experiencing the amazement of travelling off the beaten track can change the way you look at life.

We are all busy and life's excesses and extremities means that we need to take the time to reconnect with ourselves and look at some of our travel experiences with deeper purpose.

Read this book and feel enlightened and ready to travel with purpose just as Sharon lives her life. Full of light and love, always reading a good book accompanied with that compulsory glass of wine of course!

Enjoy!

Penny Spencer

Managing Director Spencer Travel

Voted one of Australia's top 30 Female Entrepreneurs 2014

Winner of Best Travel Agency Corporate – single location, Australia: 2010, 2011, 2012, 2013

Introduction

"Wherever you go, go with all your heart."

Confucius

Have you ever wondered why you have such a strong connection and great love for a certain culture, country, city or way of life? Do you have the bug and is there travel in your blood? Do you have a strong yearning to understand yourself at a deeper level, the world around you and the greater mysteries in life? I certainly have and found myself unwittingly falling into a place that was able to provide me with answers that opened up a whole new world for me.

Fate had it that my first job on leaving college was in the travel industry. I got it into my head that it would be quite a cool job. It was kind of strange really as we had not travelled a lot as a family. However, with my dad being Irish we had an instant international connection and we had lived in England and Ireland when I was very young. After a few letters to travel companies and airlines I landed my first junior travel consulting position which, in turn, initiated my love affair with travel!

The world of travel, with its sense of adventure, the connection to nature and the planet itself has proven to be the perfect playground in which to grow. When you travel with a deeper sense of purpose, off the beaten track, spending time with the wisdom keepers of indigenous groups and ancient cultures, you will receive answers to some of the greatest mysteries in life. More importantly, you have the opportunity to learn so much about yourself as you take that inner journey of self-discovery and heal at a soul level. I hear you asking me, how does this happen?

Just imagine being wrapped up ever so tightly in blankets with only your face being exposed as you lie inside a traditional Native American medicine wheel; the Hopi medicine woman singing and chanting their tribe's age-old songs above you; the drum coinciding with the beat of your heart and her voice soft and gentle just like a lullaby. Experiences like these touch the deepest part of you. You feel so alive!

Many moments of magic and experiences like this are what have compelled me to write this book and to share with those who have a love of travel and a curiosity in the spiritual side of life; the close connection between the two. As an intuitive healer, having worked with many individuals over the years, I know it does not matter from where one comes. Whether you have had a privileged upbringing or not, each person has an innate need and want to shift, change and let go of the fears that are held within. What better way to do this than travel, exporting yourself to far away spots where you get the chance to live in another culture's shoes, in a world different from your own, like that of the Hopi or Navajo as you connect with the medicine man or woman or when you find yourself having one of those "aha" moments at a sacred site, a remembering maybe, a revelation as you reconnect with a past life.

You may not believe in past lives however, you would have to agree with me, that there might have been at least one time in your life where you have been somewhere foreign and felt so incredibly at home with so much familiarity. Maybe you have met someone for the first time and feel like you have known them all your life. How does this happen? Why does this happen?

I too would have asked these same questions until that moment in my life when I visited Egypt for the first time and a series of events began to unravel, leaving no doubt in my mind that there was far more to this world than what the eye could see and far more to the makeup of myself. Igniting an insatiable hunger to delve deeper into the synchronicities that occurred and the messages received has led me to venture off the beaten track countless times with the hope that more and more would be revealed.

I have not been disappointed! I invite you to sit back, get comfortable and transport yourself with me on my magical travels to the sacred sites and ancient lands as mystery and magic unfolds.

Sharon Breslin
Author

CHAPTER ONE:

Returning Home

CHAPTER ONE:

Returning Home

Phones blasting, deadlines looming, clients waiting, staff wanting help, a back-log of quotes…Breathe Sharon, breathe!! A typical day in the world of travel, you either loved or loathed it. You either survived or you didn't. Sitting on the edge of my seat, the adrenalin flowing, not knowing what the day would bring, my eye caught an email as it popped up on my screen…INVITATION.

Ooohhhhhh…a welcome break in the chaos. Who was sending me an invite and what was it to?? Multi-tasking as usual, headset on, half way through my conversation, smiling at the clients who had just walked in the door, I clicked on the email and it opened it up. Filled with anticipation and a mix of curiosity, excitement and intrigue, I took a closer look. I'd been thoroughly spoilt over the years visiting amazing destinations around the world and had become a little blasé to 'invitations.' With my 'judgment' hat firmly in place, I thought it had better be good, but more than that, I hoped the mysterious invite was to some place I had never been before.

How ignorant of me. I know that now but at the time I took it all for granted! Over the years I had worked hard and was rewarded with some incredible perks along the way. They say "never a dull moment" and in the travel industry this rang true many a day.

"It is with great pleasure that Innovative Travel would like to invite Sharon Breslin or a senior staff member on our upcoming educational tour to Egypt. We wish to thank you for your business to date and would like to have the opportunity to show you first hand the wonders of Egypt".

Egypt, hmmm, is it a place I would choose to go to? Let me see, what is Egypt famous for? The pyramids of course and I think maybe Egyptian men who hassle girls with blonde hair. Ha, ha, ha, I laughed to myself and thought at the time, how foolish, you really know nothing much about that continent or civilisation at all. Yes this one might be worth considering. Hmmmm, I will sit on it for a couple of days. How nonchalant of me. Any thoughts of an invite, not to mention Egypt, were quickly lost as clients were brought to my desk and I focused all of my attention on their holidays and dreams. And the phones kept ringing, the deadlines loomed, clients and staff waited, quotes back-logged….. another day flew by but I think I remembered to breathe.

Life in the world of travel was all consuming and one day rolled into another. My mind continued to digest, ponder and syphon the pros and cons for the next few days. Well, I reasoned, why not accept Innovative Travel's educational invite to Eygpt? But it was such a long way to go for just a week. Should I go? I could certainly do with a break. I hadn't been to Egypt before. Oh my goodness would the business survive without me for whole a week? Oh what the heck, why not let caution fly to the wind, surely it was time for another adventure. Besides, it was time I got myself to the middle-east to learn a little more about a continent I had not visited to date. Right, go on, hit the button before you change your mind. Yes, thank you, INVITATION ACCEPTED.

Departure loomed close. Manic as usual with all of the last minute things being ticked off the list. Every travel file, notes written on, instructions left for the staff and my clients were advised that I was going to be away for a short time. Now what about me? Clothes, oh my goodness, what am I going to wear? How hot was it going to be? How much did I have to cover up when visiting the sacred sites? Will I need evening attire as well? The usual dilemmas when getting ready to depart for a foreign land. How will I fit it all in? My toiletries take up more room than my clothes! Sigh, the trials and tribulations of travelling. Even after all of these years I was still not a great "packer." Oh well, throw it all in, better to have too much than not enough. Laughing to myself I thought, well that's not such a smart way to travel, Sharon and let us not forget the compulsory shopping that you will need to squash into the suitcase for the long journey home. She'll be right! Forever an optimist I knew that if there was a will there was a way and hey it's only money after all. I could post some things home or give some of my belongings away.

The day finally dawned. Up with less than a couple of hours sleep, totally exhausted but totally exhilarated. Yahoo! On the road again, finally! The gypsy part of my soul was alive, excited and chomping at the bit for the next adventure. Business class (one of the treats for working hard and supporting the airline and supplier) would make the travelling time easier; a definite consideration given the fact that we had only a week to explore a brand new destination. It was these times that you loved beyond measure while working in the travel industry. It was the ultimate job with the most incredible opportunities. Even 20 years

down the track I still went to work every day absolutely loving it. How blessed was I? Lady luck was surely on my side.

Malaysian Airlines via Kuala Lumpur with final destination Cairo. The airline was famous for its satays with peanut sauce served with champagne and we were not disappointed. What a fantastic way to start our journey. Unwinding, de-stressing, friendships cementing as we were being transported to another place and time. Our group was made up of a mixture of leisure and corporate travel companies and everyone was frantically trying to find their place within the group; the joker, the one who was always late, the one who was always on time, the loner, the timid one and the loud one. Dynamics were forming the tight knit bond that we would create over the following week as a group of strangers coming together, to travel to one of the most amazingly mystical countries in the world. Little did we know just what a magical journey it was to become.

Arriving after a grueling 26 hours it was with relief that we gathered our bags and made our way off the aircraft into the terminal building at Cairo airport. Tired, in need of a shower and a few hours sleep to acclimatise we were hit with the chaos of Cairo airport. Wow. I looked around and there were men everywhere. Where were the women? There were men in uniform looking at you suspiciously and directing you into your respective lines to process your visa as a foreigner. There were tired looking men hunched over their brooms sweeping and cleaning the arrival hall, obviously very poor but grateful to have a job no matter how tedious. At least they got to see the many tourists that arrived in droves to one of the most famous cities in the world. The dull, archaic furniture and equipment had you wondering where on earth you had landed. I should have known after all these years of travelling that an airport can be very deceiving, especially in a country that has such extremes between the poor and rich. Over the many heads in the crowd of people we saw a welcoming sign, INNOVATIVE TRAVEL GROUP. How wonderful to be met and hastened through with an air of importance. Thank goodness, as I was really tired but full of excitement nonetheless.

Destiny was calling.....

Walid El Battouty was our guide for the next week. With his piercing green eyes and definite air of authority we instinctively knew that we had been assigned one of the best.

It seemed the crowds parted way as he knew exactly where to take us and within seconds he was guiding us with ease from the airport to our waiting coach outside.

Dust, dust and more dust. Sand, arid heat and yes, dust. Before long, the earthen colours dashed with a spot of green every so often would become a very familiar sight to us. Departing from the airport with Walid booming down the microphone, introducing us to his homeland with immense pride and passion - nothing, absolutely nothing, prepared me for my first glimpse of the pyramids.

Majestic, proud, standing tall in all of their glory, they simply took my breath away. Barely containing my excitement, my eyes devoured that first glimpse of them in the distance. I wondered how long it would be before we could get up close and personal. It was in this moment

that I knew for sure that Egypt was not a simple holiday destination but so much more. I felt so at home. A country with so much depth, layer upon layer, ready to reveal itself if you respected it. So much history contained within its soil with a heartbeat so utterly unique. I could not put my finger on it but I experienced a strange yet familiar feeling all at the same time. It was like I had come home and in a funny kind of way I knew something or someone was waiting for me. Every cell in my body felt so alive and I could hardly contain my excitement. Excitement for what, I did not know. Almost forgetting that we had just flown from the other side of the world I felt work and all its stress simply melting away as we arrived at our hotel in the Giza area for the next few nights. After checking in and finding out where the pool was we agreed to meet in the early afternoon for our first official adventure. Unable to sleep, my roommate Annie and I fell into deckchairs poolside, a cocktail in one hand and a perfect view of the pyramids as they stood in all of their glory.

All of a sudden, I had a sense that this was a precious moment in time when destiny was calling. There was a greater picture all mapped out for me and I was blissfully unaware of it for now. However, the turn of events over the next week made me look at life in a whole new way. They were the first of many life-changing experiences I have now been so privileged to experience.

“Toot, toot!” Oh no, watch out! Looking out of the coach window we were totally intrigued and flabbergasted at the traffic, the roads and the activities that we were watching. This place is crazy. Our first afternoon and we were in the midst of Giza heading towards the pyramids. There were cars old and new, horses and carts, shoe shiners, sellers of refreshments, young children roaming the streets and adults going about their business. As our coach crawled through the madness looking for a place to park we had our eyes glued to the windows taking everything in.

As we stepped from the coach onto the great Giza plateau we were bombarded with the smells, noises and colours of Egypt. Smiling, yet wary locals gathered around us – hoping for a sale. Pushing past them, we followed Walid across the open desert land to find ourselves standing below the Great Pyramid of Giza – Cheops Pyramid. Words could not describe how it felt to stand there with all three pyramids a stone's throw away. If I reached out I could touch them and feel the solidness of the brick, marvel at the shape and try to figure out how each rock had been merged together with absolutely no joins.

It felt so surreal but at the same time the surroundings seemed familiar. I had a niggling feeling of "being home" from the moment I had stepped onto Egyptian soil. How could this be as I had only been here for less than a day? Pushing these thoughts aside I tuned into what Walid, our guide and Egyptologist, was sharing with the group. A phenomenon for sure, there is no other way to describe the most ancient of the Seven Wonders of the World. Listening to the facts from an Egyptologist's point of view and at the same time absorbing the energy and listening to my inner knowing, I began to wonder how on earth they came to be here and how they had survived the test of time through the different civilisations. It was not until my second trip to Egypt that I began to accept and understand the power of the pyramids and the Sphinx at a deeper level.

Like most first time tourists to the Giza Plateau, I found myself climbing up onto the humped back of a camel, in what I hoped was the most dignified way possible, to take the obligatory touristic ride around the pyramids. Weaving our way amongst the hustle and bustle of the hawkers, pinching myself every so often to remind myself I really was there, it felt like time stood still. Back to reality with a thump, I heard a hissing noise and felt my camel lunge and drop down to its knees. Managing to slide off, keeping myself upright and dignity intact, I was grateful to have my feet firmly back on solid ground.

Eager to keep us moving and reminding us that this was a travel agent's familiarisation with an incredibly full schedule, Walid rounded us all up and announced that we were heading to one of the most famous establishments in the area, a Egyptian perfume palace. There we would learn how the ancient Egyptians had become experts in creating their oils with natural herbs and plant essences such as cinnamon, cardamom, rose, geranium and many others. Secret formulas were concocted and passed down from generation to generation, upholding the nation's reputation as some of the best perfumers in the world.

Entering the perfume palace I felt as if I had just stepped back into Cleopatra's era. There were musky smells, dim lighting and unique perfume bottles surrounding us as far as the eye could see. Come, come, come and sit down over here. We were ushered into one of the corners, offered the choice of apple tea or a cold drink and made to feel welcome. This was something we would happily get used to over the next week. Sitting on comfortable chairs around a display table, the guide who had been allocated to our group introduced himself with a smile on his face and laughing eyes. He looked like he was going to be very entertaining. Perfume bottles were opened and passed around the group and I could hear oohhss and aahhhs as we sniffed and recognised some of the most famous smells we had come to know in the perfume world. Which one do you think this is....Chanel, Gucci, Dior, Elizabeth Arden? It was fascinating to hear how certain oils were used to create these signature perfumes. Our guide started to ask each member of the group, as the perfumes were being passed around, 'What does your boyfriend like to buy for you? What perfumes do you buy for your boyfriend?' I was hoping like heck he would pass me by as I was very shy at this time and I did not have a boyfriend so asking me this question would mean that I would be put on the spot and have to reveal a little more about myself. I could feel my stomach starting to twist in knots and I just wanted to shrivel down into the floor. Luck, however, was on my side and somehow he managed to skip past me and inside I heaved a huge sigh of relief. Gosh, it was only day one and we had flown such a long distance, dropped our gear and immediately headed out to see the pyramids. Emotions were high. They certainly did not need to be ignited even more by having to talk about my love life or lack thereof!

Finishing his demonstration and leaving us with an amazing array of oils to choose from, our first purchases were made. Rose oil, lotus flower oil, Queen of the Nile oil – the names alone pulled you in and transported you back to a bygone era, one that you wanted to relive. The magic of Egypt was weaving its spell on me already. I felt alive and so happy that I had decided to take this precious week out of my business world to journey to this incredible land.

Gathering around the counter and loaded up with bottles we were all trying to purchase, our guide suddenly blurted out in front of everyone, “This girl (which was me!) is a very special lady. She almost cried before, when I was demonstrating the oils.” I could feel my face going bright red and I did not know where to look. He knew. How on earth did he know? I had certainly been on the verge of tears, hoping with all of my might that he would not ask me about my boyfriend and the perfumes associated with him. He must have skipped over me on purpose! He turned to me in front of everyone and said, “Please, if you need to talk to me while you are here I am available at any time,” and promptly handed me his business card with his contact details. He said he had been working in both Egypt and Singapore and would love to talk to me. I hurriedly paid for my perfumes, stuffed the card in my bag and escaped out into the sunshine breathing a huge sigh of relief and hoping that no one would ask me anything about this odd occurrence. It felt like he knew my deepest darkest secrets. How could he?? Was he psychic maybe? His parting words had been, ‘Do you meditate?’ I did not and told him so. He promptly followed this up with, “You might like to explore that.” I thought nothing more of it as we continued at breakneck speed to fit in as much as we could in the short amount of time that we were there.

Where to next? Before leaving the Great Pyramids and the Giza Plateau, Walid told us we must take a look at “Mena House” especially if we wanted to give our clients the most wonderful treat when visiting Cairo. Perched directly across from the pyramids, surrounded by 40 acres of verdant greenery, this magnificent old palace, now converted into a hotel, stood tall, oozing history from every nook and cranny of its elegant bones. Just imagine sitting on one of the many balconies sipping a cocktail at sunset, looking out across the vast plateau while soaking up the energy of one of the Seven Wonders of the World. Wow! Words could not describe this moment of pleasure. Beautiful pools and gardens, buildings filled with antiques and treasures flowed endlessly in front of us as we were given a fleeting look around the property. If walls could talk I wonder what stories would be shared by this spectacular grand old lady!

It was time to head back to our hotel at the end of our first day; eat and crash. Weary, hungry and not knowing what time zone we were in didn't matter. What an amazing start to our week in Egypt! I found myself realising how, in one day, I had fallen in love with everything. The colours, the starkness of the desert, the earth tones that were splashed with bursts of bright colour by way of artwork, spices and fabric. The smells of perfume, the food cooking with delicious aromas from the street stalls. The people, the children's smiles as they bombarded you to buy something for a simple dollar and the regal beauty of the Egyptian women and men. The music, oh the haunting and invocative sound of the music, it was mesmerising and impossible to stop yourself from moving to the beat. I would sleep and dream well tonight, of that I was certain.

Up bright and early, devouring a hearty breakfast with a morning view of the pyramids our group gathered together for another day of adventures. Walid had very cleverly assigned us with the name of an Egyptian god or goddess so that when we were at any of the ancient sacred sites and he was explaining and sharing knowledge on the events of history we would have a deeper understanding, having stepped into the character of each of these individuals. There was so much to absorb and retain and this was a perfect way for the group to immerse themselves in the past ancient civilisation. I had been assigned the character of Anubis who was a jackal headed god associated with mummification and the afterlife in ancient Egyptian religion. In the old kingdom he was associated with the burial of the Pharaoh. At this time he was the most important god of the dead but during the middle kingdom he was replaced by Osiris. He was the master of ceremonies, leading the deceased by the hand to the scales in the Hall of Maat during the process of the "judgement day scene." In his left hand he holds the ankh, the symbol of life. I wasn't sure that I liked being associated with the "dead" but as the week progressed I began to understand Anubis and the importance of his role in aiding a soul on its journey as it crossed over into the afterlife.

Today we were flying from Cairo to Luxor to commence our long awaited cruise along the Nile! Back at the airport, passing through lines of official paraphernalia, we boarded the aircraft for our short flight. Up in the air, flying high above the desert with nothing but flat land for as far as the eye could see, we had no idea what to expect. Even in its starkness, the desert oozed beauty and mystery. My imagination was running away with me. What must it have been like to live the life of a Bedouin, a camel trader, or a member of the ancient Egyptian military, coping with the ever-changing physical environment, living each day as it comes? It seemed to me that in one moment the desert was your ally and the next your arch enemy.

Arriving in Luxor, the ancient city of Thebes and home of the famous Karnak and Luxor Temples, it dawned upon me that this was indeed the heart of Egypt. It was no longer a political centre for Egypt but established as a religious centre after the New Kingdom era. The original name of the city was “Wase” meaning “the scepter of power.” This is where the homes of the nobles and the offices of the government were found along with the palace of the Pharoah on the east bank, not far from the city. The west bank was mainly farmland and where the mountains behind the city were used to house the great tombs of pharaohs, queens, nobles and artisans.

Boarding our cruise vessel for the next four days we were greeted by Muhammad, one of the ships stewards, like we were long lost friends. First class, first class, first class. The ship was rather luxurious, oohhh I do love working in the travel industry!! Spoilt rotten, we were, but we needed to experience it from our client’s eyes, didn’t we? Annie and I arrived at our cabin and loved all of the little touches and attention to detail. On opening the door there were our towels shaped into the most exquisite swans sitting proudly on the beds. Dropping our bags we did a quick freshen up and then we were ready to venture out to explore Luxor and the famous Karnak Temple.

You could spend days, just days wandering and exploring and discovering all of the hidden messages, incredible architecture and ancient way of life. Close on Walid’s heels, listening intently and stepping into our assigned characters once again, making sure we did not miss a beat, we entered the great Hall of Pillars at Luxor. Before we knew it, hours had passed by and the night was rolling in. I loved this part of the evening when in so many ways it felt like the city truly woke up and the magic was just starting to be spun. As the sun started to set, throwing rusted oranges and pinks across the sky, the music began to get louder as the stall-holders were touting their wares ready for a night of good business. The distant echo of the drum beat, Nubian style, intertwined with the echoing sounds of the middle-east set the scene. I was in heaven.

Searching the stalls for a bargain or two, enjoying the compliments being delivered by the lovely Egyptian men as they tried to woo me into buying at their stalls, I spotted amongst the sea of colour the perfect galabiya, a traditional Egyptian garment native to the Nile Valley . Royal Blue, braided with gold and red. Yes that would be fabulous for our galabiya night on board the cruise boat. Bartering and making sure I let them have the last word I secured it for next to nothing. This was so much fun. Please don't let it end.

Hurrying back to the cruise boat, making sure we were not going to be late for dinner on board and the evening of entertainment ahead, we found ourselves deciding what we were going to wear. By day, dust, dirt and practical clothing as you fought the challenges of the environment. By night it was like stepping into another world of lights, magic, sounds, smells, delicious food, entertainment, dancing into the wee hours, laughter and the meeting of new people all over a wine or two. One had to dress accordingly! If this was work then I think I might sign up for another decade or two!

Politely refusing Muhammad I told him, no more, there is no room left for a morsel more. Joking and laughing with him I reminded him I would not be able to partake in the belly dancing later on if I ate one more thing. Moving across from the restaurant to the entertainment area on board the ship, wine glasses in hand, we secured our table, ready for a night of fun! Even after a few days it felt like we had known each other for many years. Personal stories were being shared and friendships were blossoming. It was game night on the ship and we were being paired off to partake in the hilarity that was about to unfold.

The first game was where two people had to share the eating of a banana, each starting from one end of the banana as the music played. When the music stopped they had to stand still, a little like musical chairs. Thank goodness I was not picked for that one! The extroverts in the group had volunteered. Laughter rang out as they tried to co-ordinate all of their moves, looking sexy at the same time and of course when they met in the middle the music was played for such short spells that the kiss was inevitable!

The next game was the "mummy game" where you had to wrap your partner up in toilet paper as if they were being mummified!! You guessed it, my turn.

Always a little nervous, I stepped out onto the floor hoping not to make a fool of myself but at the same time have a crack at winning. The aim was to be as fast as you could and as neat as you could. I loved it!! What happened when I started wrapping my partner up was amazing, it was like I went into a trance and I just went round and round and round making sure that there were no gaps and that the toilet paper did not break. Wrapped in record time I paused for a moment and an intriguing

thought came into my mind. I was Anubis in this group and it was he who discovered embalming and oversaw the mummification process throughout the whole of Egypt as the lord of the underworld. Was it a coincidence that I was chosen for that game and the fact that it seemed like it was second nature to me? It was another mystical moment that was lodged in my memory bank as each day we fell into our beds, tired but exhilarated, ready for the dreamtime and the excitement of the next day and what it might hold.

I am remembered, I am honoured....

What happened next just blew me away. The following day, after a full day of exploring even more of the ancient city of Thebes and the Valley of the Kings, we were promised a special visit to the largest jewellery store in Luxor. On entering the store we were greeted with rows and rows of superb jewellery. There was gold, silver, rings, bracelets, necklaces, statues and much more. A shopper's delight and the owner's too as they saw us eager to purchase. As I entered and walked into the centre of the shop and began to look around, I was stopped in my tracks noticing that all of the young men behind the counter were laughing and it seemed they were laughing at me! I began to feel rather uncomfortable and wondered, was something stuck on my back, did I have my skirt tucked into my undies, what on earth were they laughing at? As I began to feel my face turning red and was not sure where to look I saw an elderly gentleman with a warm smile on his face inviting me over with his eyes. I moved over towards him and asked, "What are they laughing at?" He replied, "They know you." I replied to him, "No, that they could not, as I have never been here before." He then repeated, "They know you!" I in turn said, "No, definitely not, this is my first time to Egypt." He then looked me square in the eyes and said, "Yes, they know you." And at that moment I realised he was indicating that I had been here before. Not in this life but in a past life. What? This did not make any sense to me. I had spent very little time at this stage doing research about past lives even though it was something I wanted to explore. I had, instead, been doing a lot of reading since my marriage break up about the topics of healing and mediumship. He then proceeded to invite me to have a seat and look at some jewellery with him. Calling Walid over, they began conversing in Egyptian as I sat there pondering on what had just happened, still a little dumfounded. Walid turned to me and said the owner of the store, the lovely gentleman I was with, was insisting on giving me some jewellery that he wanted me to wear the following day. I was to wear it and then at the end of the day decide whether I would like to buy it or not. He pulled a ring and a chain out of a cabinet then turned to me, took my hand and called me his queen! This was getting stranger by the minute.

The chain had an Egyptian goddess on it and the ring had the face of a lion. They represented one and the same and that was of the Egyptian goddess Sekhmet. Who was Sekhmet and why did he want me to wear the jewellery? Staring into his lovely kind eyes as he put the chain around my neck and the ring on my finger I felt safe and knew that there was a reason for all of this, I just did not know what it was at present.

Sekhmet's name was derived from the word "Sekhem" which means power or might and is often translated as "the powerful one." She was closely associated with the Hathor, the goddess of joy, music, dance, sexual love, pregnancy and birth and Baast, the goddess of warfare in

lower Egypt. It was said that her breath formed the desert and she was seen as the protector of the Pharaohs leading them in warfare. Known as the warrior goddess and the healing goddess she was the patron of the physicians and healers in the ancient city of Thebes. Bearing the solar disk (an aspect of Ra) and the Uraeus (upright form of an Egyptian cobra) this associated her with the wadjet and royalty. She was mentioned in the spells in The Book of the Dead as both a creative and destructive force but above all, she was the protector of Ma'at (balance or justice), named "The one who loves Ma'at and who detests evil."

What I found quite incredible was how this beautiful man knew that I was interested in healing work. I had not told him. It was something that I was exploring in my spare time, of which I had very little while running a travel company. I adored it and was devouring many books on the topic. Was there a connection with Sekhmet being the patron of the physicians and healers? I could see some other traits that might be similar. I had very strong beliefs about balance and justice and definitely would stand and fight for the underdog if I thought they were being unfairly treated. In fact, in the world of travel you had to stand up and fight for your team and clients on a daily basis. There was no time for softness, you had to roar like a lion to be heard and to make sure that you were receiving the service needed that matched the service you were expected to provide for your clients. My staff could vouch for this! They had to put up with this behaviour of mine but hopefully most of the time it was protecting them, their clients and their work, rather than offending them. Yes, it was a known fact that when I roared you had to duck for cover as it was frightening. Even my name, Sharon, originally a Hebrew name, means "fertile plain of the desert." My mind was racing, a million thoughts, questions, pondering, what was this all about? I supposed I would find out the next day when we went back to Karnak Temple and saw what awaited me there. So I finally accepted that I was to take the jewellery and wear it the following day. On leaving the shop, I realised that out of the group of twelve, I was the only one he had singled out and asked to wear the jewellery, so surely it was not a new sales technique!

Up bright and early, another gorgeous breakfast, a walk around the deck to try and feign walking it all off and then back on the coach towards Karnak temple. This place was like a drug, the more you saw, the more you learned about it and the more you wanted. Walid was the best story-teller and he had us in fits of laughter, moments of total concentration and fired many questions seeking answers. Your imagination ran wild as you immersed yourself into the energy of the old city. Every step you took you could feel what it must have been like to live there. The beauty, the sacredness and all of it was steeped in a depth of history that touched the core of your soul; soaking it up not wanting to ever leave. Why was it that I felt so at home there? Maybe I was reconnecting with one or more past lives. There were unanswered questions to foreign feelings I was experiencing.

Skirting the outside of the temple grounds and wandering off the beaten track, all of a sudden we were in an area where there were very few tourists, only our small group and the guards that Walid was hurriedly paying to allow us to visit a cordoned off area. He turned and beckoned for us to follow. We started to weave our way through a series of gateways, six in total, until we entered the sanctuary of Ptah, then the sanctuary of Sekhmet. Dark and small with very little lighting, you had to adjust your

eyes. Once inside, you realised that there was the most magnificent statue taking up most of the space within the small chapel. Sekhmet stood tall and proud, with her striking slender body contrasting with her massive head that wore a flattened disk with a raised uraeus, the upright form of an Egyptian cobra. This is the symbol of royalty and divine authority in ancient Egypt. In her left hand she held the ankh, symbolic of life. In her right hand she held the lotus sceptre representative of growth.

She was breathtaking and the energy in this small space was intense. Standing in front of her with the light beaming from a gap in the roof, that was specifically located to allow the light of day and the moonlight at night to shine onto her face, I was mesmerised by her eyes. It was as if she was alive and looking directly at me. I stood in silence, looking directly at her and talking to her in my mind and connecting with her on a deep level. It was a precious moment and one that will be with me forever. It felt like an initiation, a reconnection back into the world of healing, as if I had been infused with Sekhmet's strength and knowledge at a deep cellular and soul level. My whole body was buzzing and a whole new world was being triggered within. It felt like it was a remembering of the past and a merging of the present.

Returning to the jewellery shop in Luxor the next day I walked in to find the owner waiting with his beautiful smile and eyes full of wisdom. "Sit down, sit down," he said. "How was your day, did you have any special moments?" Of course, he knew and I did not have to say anything but I proceeded to tell him about my visit to Sekhmet's sanctuary and how powerful it had been. Yes, yes I said, I would like to purchase the jewellery to take home to wear when doing my healing work. This was just the beginning of many unusual experiences with so much meaning, learning and significance that I was to have on my return to Egypt and future travels around the world.

The remainder of our week in Egypt was a whirlwind where we continued cruising down the Nile visiting the temples of Edfu, KomOmbo and Aswan. Along with a day trip to Abu Simbel by air and then back to Cairo for a speedy tour of the famous Cairo museum. Alas, it was over in a blink and we found ourselves at the airport saying our last farewells to Walid, thanking him for the most magnificent week. Apparently, my parting words to Walid were, “I will be back to visit you and it will be with groups in the future.” It was something that I cannot remember saying but he enjoyed reminding me of it when I next returned to Egypt.

CHAPTER TWO:
The Gift of Knowing

CHAPTER TWO:

The Gift of Knowing

It was the wee hours of the morning and I was sitting tucked up in my chair, very cosy indeed and with my meditation well under way. I had a sudden flashback to how far I had come since my return from Egypt. I was practicing what I had been asked, not once but at least three times during my visit to Egypt, and that was "Did I meditate?" On reflection, I realised that my travel to Egypt was no coincidence. It was part of a higher plan, my blueprint you could say. Stepping on to Egyptian soil had reignited the spiritual flame within me, encouraging me to explore all things metaphysical, the ancient wisdom of the indigenous groups and of course my beloved healing work. I had embraced these new discoveries and was introducing them into my working and personal life wherever I could.

Life was chaotic as usual with a maximum of six hours sleep on a good night and then up and into the day. Owning and operating a travel company was certainly challenging and exhilarating all at the same time. I had trained myself to survive on six hours sleep so that I could arrive at the office in the early hours of the morning and do a day's work before the phones started, staff arrived and clients appeared. One thing I had promised myself during this crazy regime was to make time to religiously practice my meditation before I left for the day even if it was only for ten or fifteen minutes. I saw it as a gift I was giving to myself when most of my time was fully consumed by other people and

activities. This was the least I could do to help clear my mind and gain some sanity in the fast paced life I was leading.

Trusting in my meditation miracles were revealed…

One of the first things I decided to do when I returned from Egypt was to seek out a teacher who could teach me the initial steps of meditation. I opened the phonebook and wrote down a list of places to enquire at and promptly left the house with list in hand. It was not long before I found my teacher. In fact, it was the very first place I had intuitively thought might be able to help. I loved how I was learning to trust my intuition more and more as I delved into this whole new world of metaphysics. An enthusiastic young man from Canada was offering one on one lessons in meditation. Perfect, I thought, I loved the idea of not having to do my learning in a group. This was a personal journey and one that needed to be kept as sacred as possible. He taught me no particular method and that was even more fitting as, being the rebel that I am, the fewer the rules, the better. The first thing Bobby-Joe had me do was to think of a place that I loved to be so that I could imagine it in my mind's eye and effortlessly take myself there. Needless to say, it was the Hall of Pillars in the old city of Thebes. From here I was able to learn how to travel down into a quiet place, allowing my thoughts to initially float through at a fast pace and then eventually slow down so that I could begin to listen for the messages and take note of any pictures I was being shown. Wow, this was mind blowing. A world that I knew existed but I had never been privileged enough to participate in, until now.

Each morning it became easier and faster as I sat in my chair with my feet firmly on the ground closing my eyes and sinking down into the peaceful place that meditation brings you to. Imagining a white light beaming down from above and totally covering me in the shape of a pyramid I began to feel the energy flowing in a circle around me. There were moments when I felt like I had zoned out altogether and then I would click back into the room suddenly, wondering where I had been. Had I fallen asleep or was I in a deep theta state moving between the conscious mind and the subconscious mind? Then, for the very first time, it happened! I was flying, flying at great speed, soaring through the air between the mountains over a valley and a beautiful river. I was taken down to the riverside and I saw what looked like Indian children playing. Where on earth was I? I did not know but I loved it. I felt free, with not a care in the world and life was so simple. It was an incredible feeling that I could see everything like watching a movie and the speed at which I was travelling as well, wow! How did it all work, what did it mean?

Every morning I longed for my meditation time to kickstart my day as I ventured into the world of magic. I kept being shown more and more and before long I was flying to many amazing places around the planet in my meditations. It was not until some time later that I discovered I had been astral travelling. Long forgotten practices from many past lives were reconnecting me to the way of the Shaman. My world was opening up at a great speed of knots to the ancient wisdom and mysticism as I began to explore the age-old Shamanic techniques. I was intrigued and fascinated as I learned through my own experiences and research how the indigenous cultures were able to psycho-navigate

to both distant physical locations and sources of inner wisdom. This incredible journey was happening within me and it felt like I had just woken up from a deep sleep.

Many months later, when the universe and destiny connected me with the most beautiful Incan Master, Willaru to guide my Lifestyle Journeys tours in Peru, I understood when he talked many times about the sleeping conscious. They are those who have not woken up yet.

The agency was busy and doing well with new staff on board and with an increase in sales and targets being met. Life was peachy, busy but peachy! Sitting at my desk wading through the emails and working on quotes, once again an email caught my attention. INVITATION –

> *Qantas would like to invite Sharon Breslin and partner to Buenos Aires on the 15th May to celebrate reaching the Top 10 Agency list for Qantas in New Zealand for 2001.*

Wow! Really, is this for real? A weekend in Buenos Aires, dancing the tango and salsa and shopping; I was so excited. I loved the music, the food and the culture and could not wait to go and explore. What better way to do that than with Qantas on an all expenses paid weekend. I may work hard but it was worth it when these treasures came along. The next thing, the phone was ringing and one of my best friends, Petra, who owned another House of Travel, was screaming down the phone, 'Yeah! We are both going to Buenos Aires, I just saw your name on the list!"

I am not sure who mentioned it first but it was not long before ideas were being floated about us extending our Buenos Aires weekend and heading up to Peru. We would be so close to Machu Picchu, surely we could take a week off and have a holiday together? Plotting and planning, we had an itinerary sorted within no time.

I had decided to take Linda, my business partner, and Petra was bringing her husband, David. Linda declined the offer to extend the trip to Peru so it was the three musketeers who would extend the stay and go exploring after our weekend of luxury! The excitement was building and there was a lot of hilarity in the office before our departure. The staff were throwing comments around and saying things like, "You will be travelling business class for sure, Linda, because you are with Sharon and she is a real tin bum…luck is always on her side." So I joined in playing the game and saying, "No sweeties, we won't be travelling business class we will be travelling first class!" I guarantee you. I was hoping for a miracle to prove to the staff that the power of positive thinking wins out every time. This was part of my plan to teach them how you can manifest anything you wish for if you want it badly enough.

Finally, the day dawned and Linda, Petra, David and I arrived at Auckland Airport where we were to meet up with the 16 other participants and representatives from Qantas. We were ushered straight to the Qantas lounge to be told there were four first class seats available on the flight up to Buenos Aires and that they were going to put our names in a hat and four of us would have a chance to win the seats. This was the moment, the moment where putting all of my manifesting skills into

practice would prove themselves…or not! The first name was drawn out – Sharon Breslin. Phew….a long breath was released from my mouth as I realised that I had been holding everything in with great anticipation. The second name was drawn – Petra Otte. Ha ha, we were onto a good thing. The four of us were going to be travelling first class all the way to Buenos Aires.

What a treat. On board, each of us were given our own set of pyjamas, a bag full of goodies filled with Elizabeth Arden products and our food was being prepared by our own chef! What more could we ask for? This was going to be a spectacular trip for so many reasons.

Buenos Aires did not let us down. The two days were a whirlwind of sightseeing in the La Boca, San Telmo and Recoleta areas. We were out till the early hours of the morning, practicing our salsa moves and enjoying the fabulous food and wine. What a blast! Buenos Aires was a city that would have been a very beautiful and gracious old lady in its time with so much class and culture. The architecture was magnificent, the parks stunning, a different form of street art around every corner. One moment you would be watching a mesmerising tango and the next, studying an artist painting the scene in front of you. Unfortunately, due to the economy this grand old lady was a little tired and run down in parts but this did not stop the city and its people living life to the full with great pride in their culture. Vibrant Latino charm was just oozing from every inch of this spectacular city.

It was time to say our goodbyes to the rest of the group and for Petra, David and I to carry on to Peru for our Machu Picchu adventure. Having had very little time to think about this leg of the journey, (as well as being nonchalant when it came to my own travel plans when always planning them for others), all of a sudden I realised that I had done very little research and was once again blindly trusting that all the magic would unfold in front of me.

I did not have to wait long before it began. After spending the night in Lima we were up at the crack of dawn for our early morning flight to Cusco. It was just breathtaking as we departed from Lima, which is very dry and located at sea level, and made our way to high above the snow clad Andes within a short period of time. The cloud floated below and the mountains stood before me in all of their glorious and majestic form. They were truly magnificent and such a beautiful sight that it is hard to capture their beauty in words. Around us, I could feel and sense the presence of the "Apu," the name given to the mountain spirits in Incan mythology, as we flew over the Andean mountains heading towards Cusco.

Disembarking from the aircraft I was not prepared for the sharpness of the air and the extra gulps I had to take as I found my breath more than a little shallow. I wondered how long would it take to adjust and regulate my breath so I that I would feel at ease. All of the books you read on altitude were right! Today was going to be a slow day with slow walking, resting and eating lightly. Maybe the locals had some magical potions they used to help, I hoped so!

Wrapped up warmly and moving forward with the throngs of people, a faint sound in the distance became much clearer. The pan pipes, the

haunting Peruvian traditional music, were welcoming us to Cusco. I could feel the tears welling up in my eyes as the music touched my soul and triggered so many emotions. I loved the music so much. I was so happy to be here. Collecting our bags and finding our transfer, all three of us were glued to the coach window as we headed towards the hotel. Like big kids in a candy store we couldn't help ourselves as we commented, each of us excited – look at that, oh my goodness, the colours they are so vibrant, the hats the ladies are wearing, the men with the long hair and panpipes flung across their shoulders! There was so much to see that there would be no time for sleep or slowing down!

With only a couple of days in Cusco we wanted to make the most of it. A short rest under our belt, our walking shoes securely fastened, meeting in the foyer we began to explore the town. Cobblestone streets, winding alleys, row upon row of stores selling everything from woollen products to intricate handmade jewellery. There were proud Peruvians going about their day, old woman sitting on park benches knitting, young men touting for business as they tried to entice you into their restaurants. There was never a dull moment with a surprise around every corner especially as you ventured up the steep side streets perched on the hillside of Cusco.

Inevitably we were drawn back into the main square many times during the course of our day as there was always something special to look at. In Incan times it was known as Huacaypata (Warriors Plaza). During these times it was an important ceremonial site where many of the Incan Kings built their royal palaces. Many believe that the city was originally planned as an effigy in the shape of a puma, the most sacred animal to the Incan and Peruvian people. You could only imagine how important this site must have been for the Incan people as its energy still conveyed this every time you stood in the square. Tragically, the Spanish started invading in 1553, destroying many Incan palaces, temples and buildings. As time progressed, they used the remaining walls as bases for the construction of a new city and this is the Cusco we know today with its mixture of Spanish influence and Incan indigenous architecture.

Whether we were here for breakfast, lunch or dinner, perched on one of the many balconies overlooking the square we were promised entertainment. Watching the town wake up as the sun rose over the mountains, the shoe shiners finding their spot, locals setting up stalls, school children heading to school, artists lost in their painting, business men opening up shops and the sad sight of the beggars asking for money, you never tired of the activity. Or maybe it was as the sun was setting and the air was becoming cooler, when we hurried to find a place to watch Cusco by night. With cocktails in hand, dusk on the horizon and the lights illuminating the massive cathedral, Santo Domingo in all of its beauty, accompanied by the South American beats of local musicians, we were in heaven. We all agreed that maybe we could live here. Half of us wanted to stay and the other half wanted to carry on and experience the next part of the adventure. Tomorrow we would be up early and travelling from Cusco to the Sacred Valley eventually heading towards Machu Picchu. Tired but extremely happy we said our good nights and arranged our meeting time for breakfast, before our early departure.

Yum, the smell of fresh bread, I will never tire of it. For some reason, eating local bread, cooked daily just seemed that much more delicious

and being fresh and not processed, surely it was better for us. That was my reasoning and excuse for tucking in and having a second or third helping! Never you mind, I told myself, I will walk it off over the next few days with the climbing we were going to do in the Sacred Valley.

Even though we had accustomed our bodies to the altitude in Cusco we were happy to know that we would be dropping in altitude as we arrived in the Sacred Valley. A little less pressure on the body and maybe a chance to have a wine or two!! David, Petra and I were easing into the Peruvian way of life and loving the simplicity of it all. Joking and laughing while we waited for our coach to arrive, we really had no idea where we were heading but we were eager to get on the road once again. Venturing out into new territory and the promise of visiting one of the new Seven Wonders of the World, Machu Picchu, we were eager to start exploring.

Having boarded the coach and settled in for the ride ahead we began meandering the narrow and sometimes heart stopping streets of Cusco, winding our way to an even higher altitude and the unknown. Looking back at the city, it surprised me how spread out it was. Many of the homes were half finished and my heart felt heavy as I saw the true poverty that many lived with on a daily basis. The cold hard truth could not be hidden from this angle. Even though the heart of Cusco conveyed another message, the outskirts of the city uncovered the illusion and confirmed to us just how many of the locals truly lived. Bittersweet, I was reminded of how important the tourism industry was for this third world nation. It was a tandem need - they needed us to survive and we needed them to share the knowledge, history and ancient wisdom of the Incan Empire and before that of the great Lemurian civilisation.

Stopping at Sacsayhuaman, one of the most stunning Inca ruins located on the northern outskirts of the city and the former capital of the Incan Empire, we spent the next few hours trekking around the site learning about the complex itself. Covering such a huge area it was originally capable of housing up to 10,000 men. Wow! The remains of the outstanding outer walls of the original city took my breath away; the size of the walls, the strength of them and most intriguingly, how the stones joined seamlessly together. They were huge and there was not a crack to be found between any of the stones. Odd shapes and sizes all merging into each other like a jigsaw puzzle, a builder's delight with the straightest of lines, smooth finishes and precision that was second to none. How did they do this so long ago? How did they move the large stones to get them into place? Could it be done now? It was a marvel, a mystery and one that we would forever be seeking the answers to. In that moment I was reminded of the exact same construction that was to be found in Egypt.

Was it Déjà vu or something else?....

Boarding the coach, deep in our own thoughts as the magnitude of what we had just seen sunk in, we headed once more along the winding roads towards the Sacred Valley. Tummy's rumbling we were wondering how far away lunch was. Then in a flash, all of a sudden, time stood still for me. It was like a magic spell being played out in slow motion in front of me. An epiphany! My eyes hastily soaked up all that they

could in the moment as my mind played catch up. Having reached the crest of the mountain and beginning to start our descent down into the Sacred Valley, its beauty laid out before us, I realised that this was the scene I had been taken to countless times in my meditation at home. Goosebumps formed all over my body. I gasped out loud. I could not believe the emotions I was experiencing. How could this happen? Everything was exactly the same; the river and its bends, the lush fields alongside the river where I had seen the Indian children playing and the expansiveness of the valley itself. In that moment I knew that I had been here before. Not in this life, but a past life. Words could not explain the strong sense of knowing, just knowing, and accepting that this was so. The significance and understanding I had all of a sudden, about many things, welled up inside of me. Who would have thought that practicing my 10-15 minutes of meditation each day would reward me with this incredibly special moment in my life?

An absolute confirmation of the power of meditation, I knew this was another step along my spiritual path and one to take note of. Just imagine if I committed to practicing more and connecting at an even deeper level to my soul, to all of the knowledge within, what could happen. Like someone who felt continuously hungry no matter how much they ate, I promised myself there and then to feed my soul with time and respect as I delved into this special place. In return, I knew I would receive something I could never learn in any educational institution. It was priceless, with no constrictions, bringing a deep sense of peace and understanding about the many mysteries and intricacies of life. I wondered where I would travel to next in my meditation before finding myself visiting the exact place in the physical some time into the future.

It was time to create those special journeys that I had been starting to dream about. Come hell or high water when I got back to the office I would find a way to begin taking spiritual journeys on a regular basis within the structure of my company. As I sat there and recapped what had just happened I realised that these opportunities needed to be shared. There must be so much more out there to explore, I had only touched the tip of the iceberg. The fire in my belly was fully ignited and my passion was strong. It dawned upon me in this moment, as my own spiritual growth was being fast tracked, that maybe it was my destiny to guide people to these power spots so that they too, could have similar opportunities to expand themselves beyond anything they could have imagined. The importance of spending time at ancient sites on sacred land with indigenous teachers was revealed in more depth to me as I sat somewhat stunned at the total mystique of it all. That sitting in meditation and experiencing something called astral travel momentarily allowed you to see into the past or the future, certainly into another dimension before having the opportunity to experience it in the physical. Oh there was just so much to learn…or was it so much to remember? Did returning in the physical to places around the world that you may have experienced in a past life allow the memories deep within the soul to be reconnected to the conscious mind and your physical being? I went home to immerse myself in the library and uncover more.

Little was I to know how many times I would return to Peru bringing likeminded travellers with me to share in the esoteric science and some of the metaphysical mysteries of life. It was a few months later that a dear friend of mine, Sylvia, a wonderful astrologer who had studied Mayan astrology, told me that my name meant the following. The

NAVIGATOR!! In Mayan times, at the precise moment that you were born, depending on where the planets and stars were positioned, you were allocated a name that described your mission in that life. Today we would call it our career.

There are no coincidences in life. In that moment it became clear that my job was indeed to navigate people on a journey whether it was in the physical to the many wonders around the world or internally by way of healing and spiritual teaching.

Where to next, what did the universe have in store for me??

CHAPTER THREE:

Messages From Out of the Blue...

CHAPTER THREE:

Messages From Out Of The Blue...

"Fly high, as high as you can and your gifts will be revealed." It was all rather cryptic but very exciting and powerful at the same time. We were in the last few hours of the most wonderful weekend workshop on all things spiritual. Helen, one of my dear friends, a gifted psychic and spiritual teacher, had just led a meditation and given every one of us in the group a special message from spirit and this was mine! What on earth did it mean? She had also proceeded to tell me I had been a seer in a past life in Peru!

Writing it all down and tucking it away in my journal I had a strong sense that it would not take long, when the timing was right, for it to begin unfolding and I would fully understand what seemed so cryptic to me at that moment.

Now for some, this would be dismissed as a whole lot of baloney but for those of us who believe in mysticism, the metaphysical aspects of life and spirituality this was a language we understood. It was still very early days for me when it came to this new way of viewing the world but I could not deny the fact that I had felt so incredibly at home in Peru. Running down the sheer cliff face when I reached the top of Waynu Picchu, with no fear, just like the locals, made me wonder how I could do that so effortlessly and everyone else was so scared. Had I been there before? There were so many unanswered questions but I guess this was

fitting when I thought of the often quoted, "It is not the destination but the journey." No doubt, as I delved more into the esoteric science and practiced my healing work more I would gain much knowledge on what was currently the unknown for me. It was like digging into a treasure chest overflowing with gold or a library full of the most exquisite books full of precious gems!

When the student is ready the teacher will appear...

Every spare moment I had between work, family and friends I spent trying to further my knowledge and the understanding of all things holistic. Like a small child at a fair with so many rides to choose from, it felt exactly the same for me when it came to all of the courses that were out there! Aromatherapy, reflexology, reiki, past life regression, the power of crystals, mediumship, hands on healing, the benefits of raw/living food and the list went on. Oh what to do first? There was a part of me that knew instinctively that these gifts were already within, I just had to recognise how to tap into them. Maybe a weekend workshop would allow me to do this. With my meditations well on their way and devouring every book I could get my hands on, my world was constantly being expanded. Stumbling across a gentleman by the name of Edgar Cayce was an inspiring moment for me. He became my guru. I loved everything he stood for and his work was just amazing. In my eyes, he so richly deserved the title, "The most modern day prophet of our time." I devoured his books and appreciated the dedication to his work and his lifelong commitment in being of service to humanity.

During the day he was a quiet, humble layman, earning a living as a photographer who was dedicated to his faith and family and then at night his world transformed as he entered into a trance state and delivered the most profound knowledge by way of reading for anyone around the world. All he needed was the person's (he called them, the entity) full name, date of birth and place of residence. Within moments he would tap into his medical diagnostician skills and determine the health of the subject at hand. His psychic and clairvoyant skills allowed him to access the Akashic records and provide a full report on the "entity's" personality type, traits, what to look out for if they headed down a particular path in this life and what they had brought in from their past lives by way of strengths and weaknesses. Wow! I aspired to work like that one day. His accuracy was phenomenal and that is why he was known as the most modern day prophet of our time. They documented and recorded over 14,000 stenographic records of his readings that he had given to over 8000 people during 43 years of practice. These recordings are still referred to on a regular basis around the world. A university was created in Atlanta in 1932 to preserve the readings of the pioneering Edgar Cayce and the ground-breaking work that he had engaged in so tirelessly until he passed. Known as the A.R.E – Association of Research and Enlightenment, it is a university dedicated to esoteric science, spirituality and mysticism where students can attend to further their studies.

Edgar Cayce also became an authority on many other topics such as reincarnation, religion and psychic development, mysteries of the mind and prophecy. He prophesied on past ancient civilisations, current nations and the karma attached to not only an individual but a nation, as

well as future geologic changes that will and have occurred with long lasting effects on our earth as we know it today. Later on, further down the track, having the opportunity to explore the world on my spiritual pilgrimages, Edgar Cayce's work became like a bible or reference book to me as I compared some of my own experiences with his writings.

A spilt-second decision to follow my gut instinct...

It was a Sunday afternoon and Linda and I were in the office frantically working away trying to catch up on the huge workload so we could have an easier week ahead of us. I had said to Linda, there is a wellness festival on down the road, I think I might pop over on my lunch break and have a look at what was on offer. She agreed to come with me so we headed over to the local town hall, paid our entrance fee and started wandering around the hall. I let Linda know that I was going to have a walk around, see what was there and choose one thing to do. Linda was close on my tail as we both made our way peaking over people's heads and around bodies to see what might take our fancy. In the last row I saw exactly what I wanted to do. There was a woman drawing spirit guides. That was something that I had not had done up until now and it interested me. I went up to her stall to book a time slot to find that there was only one space left and it was not until the end of the day. I turned to Linda and said, oh, I cannot be bothered and she promptly said, go on, put your name down, we are only going back to work so you can come back. I thought about it for a few moments and decided, why not, it would not be difficult for me to return and something was nudging me to do so.

Entering the town hall again later that day, there were very few people wandering around the festival and I noticed that many of the stallholders were already packing up their wares. I hoped that my lady was still there. Turning into the last row I needn't have worried as there she was still working away with a client. I hovered alongside her stall trying to be discreet but letting her know I was there at the same time. Eventually the client left and it was finally my turn. I sat down and she welcomed me and said I must be her lucky last client of the day. I explained that I had wanted to come earlier but she was obviously extremely popular and I had just managed to get the last slot.

We exchanged the niceties that you do when you first meet someone and she then switched into her own world and started drawing. I watched, mesmerised, as she created something out of nothing. A combination of pencils and crayons, yellow, blue, red and green and before long I began to see the face of the most beautiful old lady start to appear. Her eyes, they were captivating, full of compassion and understanding which made me feel that they were looking directly into my soul. The artist stopped in her tracks, looked up and asked me if I recognised the face. I said, no, I did not and she proceeded to tell me, do not worry, you will do. She then said, oh my, I am being given a name and told I must tell you. It is not often that I am given a name but I am being told this is important and the significance of it will unravel at a later date. They are telling me – "Singing Rain, Navajo." She then asked, "When you are sad and feeling down do you ever have a warm feeling spreading over your shoulders? It is her, Singing Rain, she wraps a blanket around you and looks over you especially at these times. She was a healer within her

tribe and people came wide and far to see her." The artist then turned the drawing over and told me there was a message that they (being spirit) had for me and it was as follows:

> *"You may have hidden the effects of your smoking from your family – yet, you have not hidden it from us. Most cherished daughter of the moon and stars. Follow your heart and the path will light up before you. Follow another and you will stand in their shadow. Trust – first yourself, then us."*

Really, how did this woman or Singing Rain or "they" know I smoked? I had not told the artist. A little unnerved but intrigued I thanked the woman for the beautiful drawing, paid my money and headed out to my car. What an amazing experience I had just had. It was now time to let it all sink in. Deep in thought and driving home I had another one of those "aha" moments! A profound one! All of a sudden I knew. I knew who was in the drawing and what it represented. Every night for the past few weeks when I was about to fall into a deep sleep, the face of a beautiful old woman would come so close to me as I was drifting off and in that exact moment it would feel like her face was merging into mine. So close that I could touch it and I could see her smile all at the same time. There was a strong feeling of familiarity. The conscious mind would start to switch off as I slipped into the unconscious world and explored my world further through the dreamtime. Over those past few weeks I had also experienced very vivid scenes that I woke up to in my dreams. Some time later I realised that they were very specific flashbacks of myself in past lives.

There was no coincidence that in the future my tours to Sedona encompassed a strong connection with the Navajo, working with the amazing Daniel on private Navajo land in Canyon de Chelly, Arizona. From that day on, Singing Rain has played such a huge part in my life. She is one of my teachers in spirit and also one of my main guides who works with me when I practice my healing work with my individual clients. My love and connection to the shamanic world and the indigenous wisdom keepers from around the world is where I have learnt the most valuable lessons in life thus far and for that I am eternally grateful. The messages I have been privileged to pass onto my clients, often relating to a past life, sometimes from many centuries ago in far off lands and the direct correlation to what is happening to them in this life, will always surprise and delight me. What an honour it is to explore the mysteries of life and partake in such sacred work as you become a bridge between this world and another.

Finally, the message begins to unravel....

"Fly high as high as you can and your gifts will be revealed." With Egypt and Peru under my belt, I had felt a strong pull towards Tibet for some time. Having read the "Celestine Prophecy" by James Redfield, which was based in Peru, and recently "Shambhala," another of his books based in the mountains of Tibet, I knew I had to get myself there no matter what! Known as the rooftop of the world and rightly so due to its high altitude and magnificent mountain range, the Himalayas, Tibet was full of mystique and the perfect destination to travel to if you wanted to further discover ancient wisdom while immersing yourself in the Buddhist way of life.

Stacey, a dear friend plus my right hand at work in my travel company, and I had been planning our up and coming trip to Tibet for some time. We had been plotting and planning, finally agreeing on having a few days in Kathmandu before commencing an 'Explore' two week holiday of Tibet. All booked and paid for we just had to wait for the departure date to come closer. The excitement was mounting, currency purchased and trekking gear sorted. It was not long now.

Then the unheard of happened. A day that no one will ever forget! The whole world stopped as it was shaken to its core. September 11, 2001. The twin towers were destroyed in front of our eyes and watched by the whole world while it was caught on camera and played constantly around the world on television. Over and over again. There was turmoil, disbelief, shock and fear immediately grabbing every human being by their heartstrings. Our phones were ringing constantly and people were cancelling their travel arrangements too afraid to venture out from the safety of their homes. Even those booked to travel to Australia from New Zealand were cancelling reservations. I had never seen fear and the darker side of life grip an entire world with such speed.

Working in the travel industry, we were well versed in coping with emergencies and catastrophes but this topped the lot. Stacey came to me and said that she had made a decision, she did not wish to travel to Tibet any more as we were booked to depart 10 days after this horrendous event. My heart sank. I understood why she did not want to leave but I still felt let down and afraid to step out on my own. What was I to do? We had been so excited and had spent hours planning our itinerary and the amazing experiences we knew that were waiting for us. The message kept repeating itself in my head, **"Fly high as high as you can and your gifts will be revealed."** I was scared but I knew there and then, the moment she told me, that I was still to travel. I could not let this opportunity pass me by. I was so curious as to what gifts might be revealed. I knew that the "fly high as high as you can" was very specific to Tibet, the rooftop of the world. No time to think about it any more, just tidy up your work-load, pack your bags and get on that plane!

Having practiced the power of manifesting for some time, I had, from the moment I found out that Stacey was not able to travel with me, begun seeing myself arriving in Kathmandu having made friends with the person I was seated next to on the flight from Singapore or with someone that I would meet on arrival. This person and I were going to spend a couple of days together in Kathmandu before the tour started. Trust, I was being asked to trust.

Arriving at Kathmandu airport I whisked myself through customs, having collected my bags, and taking a big breath I thought, right, this is it. I needed to find a taxi and get myself into the city and delivered to my hotel.

Exiting the airport I was hit with a sea of faces, all men and all of them screaming at me trying to get me to purchase a transfer, a sightseeing tour or a hotel reservation from them. Welcome to Kathmandu, Sharon! I thought, this is going to be interesting! Striding forward and acting braver than I felt, I hailed a taxi, bartered a price and watched while the driver loaded my suitcase into the boot. I then jumped into the car and was just about to close the door when, at the last minute, a young local

man jumped in beside me. I looked at him and thought, what a cheek! How did he think he was going to get away with invading my taxi ride? Then I became a little scared, were they going to drag me down some country road into the mountains never to be seen again? Just as I was digesting my worst thoughts he gave me a large smile and my fears melted away. "Welcome to Kathmandu," was his greeting. "Thank you," I said. He then proceeded to introduce himself and ask if he could show me around his city for a few days. He did not ask for any money so I was rather suspicious but I wondered if this was the person I had so furiously been trying to manifest, so that I was not alone before my tour started. Maybe it was.

In a split second, a decision was needed. Did I trust him and did I take him up on his offer to take me around the city on his moped? Why not, life is an adventure and here was one being presented to me on a platter. Fabulous. Yes, it felt right.

Before I knew it, bags were checked in, face freshened up and I was down in the lobby waiting for my new friend to collect me.

Heading out into the car park with him, there was our mode of transport, a moped! Oh my god, was this going to be a good idea after all? Clinging onto Sanu for dear life I closed my eyes and prayed to Allah. Where on earth are all of the cars, mopeds, bikes and people coming from? This place was stark raving mad, especially when it came to road rules or lack of them. After ten minutes or so I began to relax a little as I felt my body move with the motion of the bike and my grip lessened a little. Finally, I was able to actually take in what I was driving past and start to enjoy a city that was full of colour and vibrancy! Zooming here there and everywhere, Sanu showed me around the major historical sights of the city, some of the vast array of stalls selling everything you could imagine and of course we ended up at a fantastic rooftop restaurant where we shared a curry, glass of wine and a story or two while we watched the sun set over Kathmandu and the city transition from day to night. How lucky was I to have met Sanu and see the city in a way that I could never have imagined and not have to pay anything for it!! I was so glad I had trusted myself enough to follow through on my next adventure and come to Tibet. It could prove itself to be the best one yet!

Sitting around the large table in the hotel I was observing the group while I listened to our Explore guide as she introduced herself and then continued to go over the housekeeping rules for the next couple of weeks while we were on tour. First impressions always make an impact. Looking around the group I automatically began to guess and build a story in mind as to what each person did, whether they were one of the loud ones or one of the quieter ones. Which ones would I get on with best? I presumed everyone else was doing the same to me. It turned out that we had a mixture of nationalities: English, Australian, New Zealand, Brazilian and South African. It felt good to finally be with the group and we were all so chuffed to be there after the world events of the past few weeks.

Funnily enough, the moment you entered Kathmandu and Tibet you had absolutely no idea what was happening in the outside world and that was the way it stayed for the whole time we were touring. It taught me that the media certainly put the fear of god into us all and it was

often just bad luck if you were in the wrong place at the wrong time. I vowed and declared to myself that I would not buy into any more of this fear mongering behaviour and not let these events stop me from travelling. In fact, I learnt that it was often the safest time to travel to a destination, just after an attack, as the security was stepped up and the city or country was desperately appealing to the tourists to return at this time, welcoming them with open arms.

I had been roomed with the Brazilian girl and after the first night or two I began to wish that I had my own room. As social as I was, I loved my own space and I really wanted to be able to meditate. Then a brilliant thought hit me. Of course, Stacey and I had paid in full for our tour and we had reserved a twin room. Working in the industry had its advantages and knowing the logistics I realised I was still entitled to that room even if Stacey was not there as there had been no refund given to Stacey. Currently, Explore had saved themselves the expense of an extra room but officially they had been paid for it and I decided I was going to try and have it. They accepted my explanation immediately and miraculously I had my own room for the rest of the tour! How grateful I was, as I could now do my meditations. Unbeknown to me, these meditations were to become so important over the next couple of weeks.

It took us a few days to get used to the food, having been absolutely spoilt in Kathmandu. After the first couple of meals we had begun to wonder how much weight we might lose as they were pretty tough to stomach. The cookies and crisps that I had managed to find were looking pretty good at this stage! Adjusting to the altitude, the Chinese influence in Tibet and the way of life was starting to take its toll on a few in the group but before long we got into the rhythm of things and a few days later we even found fresh vegetables, rice and home baked bread. Life was looking up! These fundamentals are so very important to get right when travelling. It makes for happy people!

Each day we never tired of staring out the coach window as we drove for miles upon miles up incredibly steep mountainsides dotted with Tibetan prayer flags and stone offerings, past lakes that were so blue they took your breath away, only to discover a remote village around the next bend and as soon as the bus was heard the children came running. Observing and accepting the nomadic way of life took some getting used to. Seeing the harsh conditions these resilient people lived under really got you thinking about how lucky we are - or are we? Weathering the elements and void of technology, you could not deny the fact that the Tibetans were happy. The faces looking back at you were worn but at the same time they were stunningly beautiful, displaying a true sense of peace and tranquility. How often did you see that in the west? Their deep connection to their faith, the importance of the monasteries and the understanding that it was an absolute honour to live the life of a monk was blatantly obvious for us to see. They could teach the western world with all of its money, fast cars and wealth a thing or two. Where had we gone wrong? Time and time again, as we mingled with locals we saw how none of the material things in this world guaranteed true happiness.

Alone in my room I began to practice my meditation morning and night and it was not long before the most incredible thing started to happen. I would close my eyes and fall into a deep meditative state and the next

thing I was flying through the ether being shown scenes that were so real as I was observing colours, buildings and people. It immediately dawned upon me that I was being shown where we would be going to on the next day of the tour!! No word of a lie, each day I knew beforehand what I would be seeing. I kept this to myself, it was my little secret, but I was bursting at the seams wanting to discuss this with someone!

The penny finally dropped, I had brought myself to Tibet and immersed myself in the purest of energies and by flying high, as high as I could, my gifts were being revealed, my third eye was fully opening and beginning to reactivate itself.

My heart sang and my soul cried with joy as I took another step in my spiritual journey. I was beginning to realise my purpose and how I was to use these gifts in this life.

I remembered something very significant that one of my dearest friends, Linda George, an accomplished astrologer had told me. She quoted Steven Forrest, an American astrologer, to me when we were looking at my chart – "instinct will guide you back (in your travels) to that busy marketplace, or the "scene of the crime," providing you with the chance to heal a hurt or renew a past strength." In other words, returning to a part of the world where I may have had a past life would be cathartic and could be very liberating at the same time.

Having made our way overland from Tsetang we spent many days visiting the most beautiful monasteries where we got to experience the life of a monk firsthand as we were taken through their daily routines. They worked very hard and there was great emphasis put upon their academic skills. It was of the utmost importance to study and to continuously improve and embrace their wisdom through learning. As I discretely watched the monks praying, chanting and meditating, I never stopped marvelling at the treasures that the monasteries housed. There was gold, gold and more gold, tapestries, paintings, candles, intricately painted furniture and of course the statues representing the gods that were so important in the Buddhist faith. Humbling and thought provoking I was pulled into the present and the hilarity on the bus. There was much chatter amongst everyone as we were finally going to arrive in Lhasa that day; the city we had all been waiting to get to!

We were not disappointed! Arriving at our hotel we were thrilled to see we were staying in one of the more traditional buildings and not one of the modern eye-sores that were scattered around the city centre. It was only a stone's throw from our door to Barkhor square and the Jokang Monastery, the heart of Lhasa. Dumping our bags and throwing on another coat because it was freezing outside, I joined my mates, Ruth and Gavin and we ventured out into the city for the first time.

From an architectural point of view it was truly stunning to see so many of the traditional buildings all in one place. What a fine city it was.

Walking around the Jokang Monastery, viewing the open air stalls selling spices and local foods and other delicacies was great fun. By now I was used to seeing half a cow or some kind of animal being tucked under a Tibetans arm as they went about gathering the rest of their shopping to take home and feed the family. There were old faces and young faces going about their business and many of them with their

prayer wheels in hand as they walked in deep contemplation. It was such a natural activity especially around the Jokang Monastery where I soon became aware that they had specifically chosen to walk around this sacred place of worship as they recited their prayers internally. The Tibetans believed that by walking and reciting their prayers at the same time you exercised the spiritual, mental and physical aspects of yourself. Then there were the even more serious ones who were focusing on their prostrations, a particular yoga type move, with gloves on their hands to soften the impact of doing more than I could count. Such dedication and discipline! These activities, practiced in public by young and old, exhibited that the Tibetans were very much aware of something called balance and faith as they engaged in the traditional ways. I wondered how long this would be allowed as I thought about the atrocities that were happening to this nation and the never-ending fight for freedom. The karma of a nation is continuously playing out at a subtle or not so subtle level. I began to ponder on how this would be affecting both Tibet and China currently and in the future.

The next few days were full of fun and enlightenment as we explored every nook and cranny of the city. First of all, we visited the Sera University Monastery, well known for its scholarly learning and famous "Monk Debates" that facilitated better comprehension of the Buddhist philosophy. Each afternoon in the debating courtyard you could watch the monks, both the questioner and the defender in action. With plenty of rules and a set procedure to follow it became mesmerising as the sea of crimson and yellow in front of you was pure entertainment. Their loud voices echoing around the courtyard making sure that they were getting their point across and then the slapping of the hands as they delivered their strongest views were brilliant. If we only understood Tibetan we would have learnt so much. It did not matter too much as we soaked up their passion for their topic and the healthy energy that was being exchanged between the monks.

Then it was time to visit the Potala Palace one of the most famous sights in the whole of Tibet. It is an incredible example of Tibetan architecture, perched 3,700m above sea level high on the side of a mountain. Up until 1959 it was the home of the Dalai Lama, until he fled to India during the Tibetan uprising. There were certainly no expenses spared with luxurious rooms, complete with exquisite furniture, carpets, paintings and artifacts. We spent hours wandering the grounds and exploring the palace rooms to get a feel for what it must have been like in the days when the Dalai Lama was in rule. Immersing ourselves in the history and culture of Lhasa, highlighted the essence, the flame, the knowing that this wise and cultured race have lived with and by for many years. Another culture may not have endured what the Tibetans had endured with the same grace, strength and depth of understanding that they have displayed throughout constant turmoil, to the world.

Another day over and back to the hotel to rest up before we took ourselves back to our favourite restaurant located just off Barkhor Square, Snowguns. It was very traditional, with a beautiful fireplace inside to keep us warm from the harsh conditions outside. We gathered together to share a night of storytelling and indulging in our new favourite tipple – Chinese brandy! By this stage of the trip the barriers were coming down and people were allowing their true selves to emerge. Coming together as strangers, there was no doubt we would depart as firm friends.

It was our last day in Lhasa and we were heading out to visit Ganden Monastery located on the outskirts of Lhasa, 4,300m above sea level. Staring out the coach window I was appreciating the stark beauty with the contrast of the earthen mountain colours, the brightness of the blue sky and then in the distance one tree, standing alone, a spot of colour on the horizon. It was so very simple, but oh so beautiful. I was going to miss this. Deep in thought, I could not help but think about the many similarities that there were between Egypt, Peru and Tibet. The people and the shape of their faces, either round or chiseled, the way in which they farmed the land, the land itself in parts, the jewellery and especially the colours, the homes and how they were built and much more. Had the lands once been joined together many thousands of years ago? To me it felt like they must have been and that the three countries were connected energetically in the shape of a triangle that held great significance. Why, I was not sure. Maybe it was from past civilisations and the mystery schools that once operated around the world or was it sacred information that was stored within the pyramids of each land? There were many questions unanswered and ones that I would inevitably spend my life investigating, trying to understand them at a deeper level.

Shaken from my thoughts I saw that we had begun climbing the very steep winding road up to the monastery where it stood on the peak of the mountain. It was huge and once again you wondered how on earth they managed to build such a structure with no mode of transport to haul the materials up the mountain. Wandering around the site with the local monks, weaving our way through the many solid doors that surely must have been built by giants, I felt very much at home. Laughter rang out and plenty of banter was heard amongst the young male students who were walking the grounds on their way to a class or to complete a chore. All of a sudden I had this immense urge to leave the group and just run, yes run all the way down the mountain to the bottom. I said to the tour leader I was going to meet them at the bottom, I felt like walking down. Next thing I was off, I could not stop my legs from pounding one in front of the other. No chance of a walk, I was running. Running down the mountain like it was the most natural thing in the world. I felt so free and full of life. In that moment I knew I must have done this before as the urge had been too strong and it felt oh so familiar.

I was ever so grateful for all of the messages that had been falling across my path. Learning to listen and follow through on them had allowed me to grow as a person, trusting my intuition as I began to dig deeper while researching the information I had received. Through all of this it had become clear that I was to finally follow through on my dream and create my first "spiritual tour." Of course, it was to be to Egypt where, through my own personal experience, my spiritual path had been reignited. I was so excited. Amazingly, I had 10 participants booked and ready to go! I could not wait.

CHAPTER FOUR:
Egyptian Magic

CHAPTER FOUR:

Egyptian Magic

There he was, standing tall and regal, Walid, our tour guide for the next twelve days. Commanding authority at all times you certainly paid attention but his eyes gave him away. He was a fun loving soul who was so proud of being Egyptian and sharing everything and more, about his homeland. One of the youngest practicing Egyptologists, he was also Vice President of the Egyptologist's Association of Egypt. As if that was not impressive enough, he had also been a pilot for Egypt Air in his earlier days. This was one talented man and it was great to be back on tour with him. We knew that we were in safe hands and we were in for a treat as he entertained and delighted us with his knowledge, enthusiasm and charismatic ways throughout our next two weeks together.

Was I really standing back here in my beloved Egypt with my own group of clients? Yes! I was. My dream had come true. This was my very first official "spiritual" or "holistic" or "personal development" or just outright "awesome" tour. Finally, I was getting the chance to share an exploration of the mysteries of life in one of the most magical corners of the world, with others. Hidden messages lay everywhere in this ancient land. There were messages that pertained to how it once was and messages pertaining to the individuals who had returned once again, to the energies of Egypt and previous lifetimes.

Pushing our way through the crowds we managed to get through customs with great speed and were standing waiting for our bags before

we headed to the Giza Plateau where we were to be based for the next few days. It never ceased to amaze me just how much I learnt and will continue learning each time I take a group on tour. Right from the very start, back in New Zealand, one of my clients was obsessed about the safety of her suitcase. On the journey over, there were many times that I heard her say, 'I hope my suitcase arrives in one piece.' Murphy's Law, it happens every time; the one and only suitcase that was damaged was hers! At least it arrived. On another tour I had a client with a similar fear and the suitcase did not arrive at all!

These journeys were far more than an opportunity to explore ancient wisdom and forgotten civilisations. They were an opportunity to explore ourselves on all levels, starting with our thought patterns, beliefs, actions and fears. The personal development and spiritual growth that weaved its magic within every participant in the group, throughout every moment of every day, was such a privilege to watch and to be a part of. It was life changing in every sense of the word! One participant came to me so many days later and asked, "Sharon, what does it mean when you see pictures like a movie?" The change in this woman had been incredible. From a scared and shy woman who wore baggy clothes with her money belt tied tightly to her waist and at all times, paranoid about losing things, having suitcases damaged and totally full of fear, to a woman who had discarded her money belt in favour of gorgeous carefree summer dresses. She was now smiling and laughing, cracking jokes with a fabulous sense of humour and to top it off, she was a woman who was experiencing her gift of clairvoyance for the first time. My heart sang as I saw her blossom, knowing that this was a moment in time that would change her world and her outlook upon it forever and definitely for the better. I had been reminded once again just how healing these journeys could be.

After resting and adjusting from the long flight, everyone was up early, fresh and full of awe that the pyramids were within their reach. So close! Teasing them just a little longer, I told them their first visit to the pyramids would not be until this evening when we would attend the famous light and sound show. In the meantime, today we would be travelling across the Egyptian desert to the famous Sakkara Pyramids located in what was the first capital city of Egypt. Along the way we would be making some essential and compulsory stops. These were destinations where we would learn about some of the most well known Egyptian traditions and at the same time we would have a chance to support the local economy! Shopping!! The ladies eyes lit up at this.

First port of call was a carpet factory where we were shown how the carpets were created from the beginning to end stages. It was very difficult for us to comprehend the child labour that we were seeing at every corner we turned. Walid soon put us right though. He explained that they were the lucky ones. The children we saw seated at the large looms, their fingers working at the speed of light, had been taken off the street. They were fed, housed and paid. Travelling in a third world country surely opened our eyes and touched our hearts in so many ways. If only you could just scoop them up in your arms, whisk them back home to shower them with loads of love and most importantly, hope. I suppose they did look happy though. Their big brown eyes staring back at us, the foreigners, huge smiles on their faces and loving it when we singled one of them out to praise their work. Needless to say, after much hilarity, as we engaged with the suave, charming and bartering Egyptian salesman, there were plenty of carpets either being stored on the bus or if too large, beginning the process of winging their way across the waters to New Zealand and Australia.

Microphone in hand, Walid's voice boomed down the bus, "Out to your right, look out to your right!" Cruising along one of the main highways he was trying to bring to our attention to a camel train that was forming in the distance. All we could see at first was sand, dust and a strong heat haze and then we spotted them. There were maybe 6-10 camels, each and every one of them being ridden by a person who was fully dressed in white, with turbans wrapped around their heads covering themselves up as much as possible from the piercing heat. These harsh conditions were once the way of life for so many in years gone by. As a tourist you can now take this trip from Cairo to Sakkara. One for the adventurers out there!

Stepping back in time...

Arriving at Sakkara our group was so excited. This was their first chance to walk amongst the ruins, the reality sinking in that we had made it to this exotic land. From the moment we stepped off the bus, Walid began his storytelling, capturing each and every one of us as we were given our characters from Egyptian mythology to play. Hanging off his every word, just like the pied piper, he led us from one part of the historical site to another. Questions fired back and forth and with his explanations we found ourselves transported back into the times of Ramses the II and the great kingdom that once was. How on earth could you travel these lands without a guide? I saw many other tourists with their lonely planet book at hand as they read and tried to imagine history. Nothing could replace the depth of knowledge a guide had to offer at sites such as these. I was so glad we had Walid as our official Egyptian guide. He was proving to be a hit all round.

Standing at the base of the pyramids in Sakkara I wrapped my white muslin scarf loosely around my head to block out the heat that was growing stronger every minute. As I did so, something made me look down at my calves and feet. I could not believe what I was seeing. On both of my legs just above the ankles there were two absolutely evenly spread circles in the shape of, dare I say it, what looked like shackles! What was happening? I did a double take and looked closer, calling my travelling companions over to ask them what they thought it might be? Was I going mad? How on earth had they just appeared with not even so much as any physical warning at all? There was no pain attached to the markings on my legs but nevertheless, the markings were there, for all to see. Day one and already strange things were beginning to happen. The fact that the markings were exactly the same in measurements and colour on both legs was fascinating in itself. Two rings on both legs spaced equal distances apart embedded into the skin a darker shade than the rest of my body.

I knew a little about cellular memory and I was beginning to wonder if this is what might be happening within my physical body. Wow, really? Thinking out loud I said, "If we are a soul having a human experience then my human body which contained my soul would carry its blueprint

and history with it at all times. " Could it be that I had indeed lived in Egypt in one or more lifetimes past and by taking myself back to stand on Egyptian soil once again, I was reconnecting or triggering and collaborating with my cellular memory to those times.? Unbelievable. It is one thing to read about it but to see it play out in real life was something else. It was mind blowing. These markings stayed with me for the entire duration that I was in Egypt and they promptly left my body the day I departed Egypt. At the very end of the trip, one of my travelling companions came running up to me and said, "Sharon, I know what the markings are!!" "Really!?" I said. Having tried to fathom it out and come to the conclusion that I must have been a prisoner of some sort, I was intrigued to hear her thoughts. "Look, look," she said. "All of the papyrus paintings and Egyptian carvings that we see of Royalty have one thing in common." "What is that?" I asked. "They all wear copper bracelets around their ankles!"

With the adventures of day one still unfolding we found ourselves sitting under a balmy night sky having just eaten a delicious traditional Egyptian meal of fresh vegetables, falafel, olives, dips and a selection of meats and we were now watching one of the most spectacular sunsets with the pyramids as our backdrop. Could life get any better? Yes, of course! Sitting in the first couple of rows amongst a few hundred people we waited with anticipation for the famous Giza Plateau light and sound show to commence. There was something to be said about your first, up close and personal sighting of the pyramids being at night.

With the haunting Egyptian music blasting through the open-air speakers setting the tone of the show that was about to explode in front of us, I closed my eyes and felt myself beginning to be transported to another world.

Where was I? What was I seeing? Was this for real? The laser light show had started and a strong deep sounding Egyptian voice was bellowing out into the night sky drawing everyone's attention to the spectacular view in front of us. Coloured lights rolled softly then quickly over the pyramids brightly illuminating the Giza plateau. Simply stunning, breathtaking and totally mesmerising! Here we were, sitting under the milky-way with thousands of stars shining brightly, Orion's belt very obvious up above and I was being shown through my third eye what was happening underneath the Great Pyramid of Cheops.

I did not know how to explain it to myself, let alone anyone else, but having learnt to trust my clairvoyant gift and intuitive skills I knew that what I was being shown was not make-believe. It was like looking down a telescope into another realm, one that was not physical, but one that existed in a higher dimension. There was a hive of activity in what looked like a very large room. Not any old room but a room full of computers and highly advanced technology. It was the heart of an operational centre where scientific, astrological and mathematical activities were being monitored and recorded. Next thing my attention was being drawn to the Sphinx and I was being shown many corridors beneath the sphinx with doors leading to secret tunnels. Whoa!!! I wonder what this all meant? It felt so real.

The funny thing with me is that I had never studied history at school and when I travelled I never researched. I liked to follow my instincts and

always read about a destination when I returned to my home country. I was totally unaware of the many topics of discussion about these exact things I had been shown until much later. In hindsight, years later, I am now aware that it is exactly as it is meant to be. As I have no preconceived ideas due to lack of study or knowledge the purity of what I am being shown, whether it be at a sacred site or with a client on the healing table, is just that. At the time though, it blew me away, rocked my socks off and blasted me into a whole new world of discovery!

Was what I saw from Atlantean times maybe, or was it happening then in a realm that we cannot see on a physical level? So many thoughts about why, how come and what does it all mean?

Half way through the light and sound show, deep in awe but still in my meditative state, I was rudely interrupted by a piercing scream echoing through the air. What the heck? That was too close for comfort! Oh my god, it was one of the ladies in my group. Guards were running from everywhere and other members of our group were gathering around Pam making sure she was okay. The guards were trained to look for terrorists or any untoward activity so it was no wonder that they were closing in on us, wanting to whisk her away without scaring the other tourists. Now this is going to seem weird but what actually happened was the light and sound show was focusing on the face of the Sphinx for the first time. We could clearly see the face of a lion with its nose missing. To this day, Pam, a beautiful lady, very sensible, a teacher, articulate and with great poise cannot explain what happened. Deep within her this piercing scream rose from her belly and escaped as she saw the Sphinx and its decapitated face. She is the last person you would ever have imagined to have acted like this. She prides herself on her wisdom and grace being someone you would describe as being very controlled, certainly not emotionally unstable. Why did this happen, where did it come from? She was notably shaken and could not stop crying. It pained her deeply to see the decapitated face of the sphinx and she realised in that moment that somehow she was connected to the sphinx at a much deeper level than she could explain or rationalise. Day one and all of this had happened! This was going to be one hell of a trip. This spiritual pilgrimage was going to expose us to many esoteric mysteries with very personal connections as we ventured down this sacred journey of learning and remembering. The power of travelling to these ancient lands with a purpose, even if it is unknown at a conscious level, was beginning to sink in as we reawakened the cellular and soul memories.

Memories triggered once again ....

Still in a little bit of shock from the events of the previous day, it was a slow start to the day with a delicious breakfast, much laughter and discussion as we tried to fathom out as a group just what our time in Egypt was all about.

Walid strolled into the restaurant dressed in his familiar safari pants and jacket, ready to take us back to the Giza Plateau to spend time at the pyramids in broad daylight. Sheepishly Pam boarded the bus cracking a joke and warning him to be prepared for what might happen. He rolled his eyes and took it all in his stride.

Luckily for us, the number of tourists did not seem as many today as we weaved our way past the perfume shops, down the potholed streets to park up outside the pyramids once again. Stepping off the coach we were greeted by shoe shiners and young children trying to sell candy or drinks and camel owners trying to sell rides. We took it all in our stride as we followed our wonderful leader, Walid. Listening intently to his tales he was a mine of information on the Egyptian history that he was sharing freely with us.

My personal antenna was on high alert after having had the day that we'd had yesterday. It was all part of guiding a group and I was learning that my job entailed far more than making sure rooms were okay, transport arrived on time and the food was satisfactory. It was my job to do what was called "hold the space" for my clients while on their spiritual quest and assist in teaching spiritual law wherever it was needed. Sure, it had its challenging moments but I just had to take them in my stride. I loved it as I always found myself growing and learning at the same pace as everyone else.

Today we had private time booked to enter the King's Chamber. We did not know what to expect but an adventure for sure! Approaching the entrance, the fun and games began. Christine wanted so badly to be able to enter but her body would not let her. She was petrified to enter just in case she experienced claustrophobia and could not get out in a hurry. I wondered if this was another past life connection or just her fear of being in confined spaces.

A beautiful old Egyptian man dressed in his white galabiya greeted us at the entrance and beckoned for us to follow him as we began to climb a long set of stairs. It was such an incredible feeling, standing inside the pyramid chambers. It was smaller with far less space than I would have thought which became more noticeable the higher we climbed in our ascent towards the King's Chamber. I fleetingly thought it was a very wise decision of Christine's to stay outside in the sunlight and view the pyramids from the outside. Quietly taking one step in front of the other all chitter chatter stopped as we embraced the experience and began to drift off into the world of speculating what it would have been like in ancient Egyptian times. We were feeling the energy and understanding the significance of the single file and procedure as we approached the chamber, just like the priest and priestesses would have done in ancient times. You could have heard a pin drop. Upon entering there was a magical beam of light hitting the centre of the chamber and the remains of the rose quartz crystal sarcophagus that stood prominently in the heart of the space. Everyone knew instinctively to find a spot, either sitting or standing and take some time to close ones eyes and meditate. It felt like you were in a secret place where angels and goddesses must have lived. A place to escape to that was safe, serene and peaceful. Next thing, I heard someone singing and oh, the acoustics, they were stunning. Time drifted by as I sat in this precious place contemplating what an amazing honour it must have been for the priests and priestesses who were chosen to work in the King's Chamber

Eventually descending the many stairs it was a relief to see daylight ahead. As wonderful as it was to spend time in the King's Chamber it was equally as awe-inspiring to get out into the broad daylight and

see the pyramids from outside where the sheer ingenuity of them never ceased to amaze.

Following Walid our pied piper, we headed towards the Sphinx. Upon arrival, once again the size of this incredible structure took your breath away. It was truly massive. Walking through the corridors surrounding the Sphinx we suddenly came across a place that seemed quiet and next thing Walid was paying one of the guards to give us some precious private space, to keep the tourists out while we had a chance to sit and meditate. Closing my eyes I felt the familiar feeling of drifting off into another place and time. Only, this time it seemed to happen so fast. At first you would feel a little conspicuous with other tourists around knowing that they would be looking at you. Some would be making a joke about you sitting and meditating and others, well I knew they wished they could join in. No matter whether you were spiritually minded or not just being in Egypt and spending time at the ancient sites would have been triggering things and shifting each and everyone's internal energy flow. Having the opportunity to meditate gave you an even greater chance to experience this energetic flow and reconnection.

In my meditation I was being shown the pyramids and a river or water running alongside them with a hive of activity happening on the river itself. There were large wooden sailing boats that were long and slim carrying many men on board and who were busy navigating their way as close to the side of the Great Pyramid as possible. With plenty of cargo to offload they were steering the boats with great precision so that they were able to park below the long ladders that were at the base of the pyramid that lead up to the top chambers. It was the scene of bustling times, of a dynasty that was thriving while being ruled with great clarity.

As our meditation time came to an end and we gathered as a group to discuss what each had seen or felt I was pondering on the fact that there was no sign whatsoever of the river Nile flowing alongside the pyramids anymore. I wondered what happened. Was I seeing things correctly? It was not until many years later that I was made aware of the debates over water levels and erosion levels in regards to the Sphinx and the Pyramids. I was very lucky to meet one of the most entertaining men, Anthony John West, now well into his 70's who has spent his life dedicated to researching these theories having travelled to Egypt more times than I can recall. An author, lecturer, tour guide and much more I found myself sitting with him in a traditional New York Deli back in 2008 hanging onto his every word. His knowledge and the ability to tell a story was fascinating. He had me sold and I found myself hoping that one day he and I would travel to Egypt and explore the mysteries together.

Adventures on the Nile...

As we bid our fond farewells to Cairo and the Giza Plateau we began winging our way to Aswan in Upper Egypt, I was excited to be returning to one of the most vibrant cities on the Nile. Famous for its African influence by way of music and dance I was so looking forward to exploring the city once again. With music in my bones and a love of dancing, the beat of the drum took me on a journey every time. If there was a drum playing there was no stopping me, I was up and practicing

my shimmying, laughing and clapping and encouraging everyone else to do the same! Driving from the airport to our hotel, which was located on its own island on the Nile, I caught glimpses of the colourful markets with rows and rows of spices, trinkets, antiques, galabiyas and t-shirts that were for sale with plenty of bartering to be had.

A short ferry ride across to the hotel and we were all checked in, bags dropped and ready to head out for the day to visit first, the Temple of Philae and later in the day, Agatha Christie's hotel room at the Old Cataract Hotel where she resided for many months while writing one of her most famous books – Death on the Nile.

The Temple of Philae plays such a significant part in Eygptian history. They say it is where Isis brought the remains of her murdered husband, Osiris, and that her tears of sorrow created the Nile itself. Isis, known as the goddess of magic and wisdom and the personification of the "complete female," was called the "One who is all" and the "lady of ten thousand names." Tricking Ra, the sun god, who originally was the most powerful to reign in the ancient world, she became the most powerful of gods and goddesses over that time. Isis had mixed some of his saliva with mud to create a poisonous snake to bite Osiris. He eventually agreed that if she cured him he would reveal his secret name, which was the source of his power over life and death. Reluctantly, due to the pain he was suffering, he whispered his name to her, Ra, as she performed her magic and healing. At this precise moment Isis became the owner of his power of life and death becoming the most powerful of the Egyptian gods and goddesses utilising her great powers to benefit the people.

Walking around the Temple of Philae there was a great sense of peace and calmness. With the soft breeze floating off the water, lightly brushing my skin, the sun shining, the beautiful gardens and monuments to stroll through, it felt like I had stepped into a place of magic. The group dispersed and found themselves a quiet spot to sit and think, write in their journal or meditate and soak up the beauty and essence of Isis herself.

Leaving the peacefulness behind we jumped onto the boat to head back to the hustle and bustle of Aswan. Nubian drummers played for us while we skimmed across the water and there was much laughter and hilarity as we tried to shake those hips while travelling at quite some speed! Back on the bus and once again winding through the streets of Aswan on our way to the Old Cataract Hotel you could not help but notice the local people going about their daily lives and wondering if it had changed much from years gone by. Still commuting by donkey, drawing carts full of their worldly goods, dressed in leather thongs and galabiyas you might think not. Then around the next corner you would see a five star hotel with all of the trimmings and realise that you were indeed in the 21st century.

Upon entering the Old Cataract Hotel, I was immediately in Agatha Christie's shoes in my mind's eye, imagining what it must have been like in the late 1920s staying at this grand hotel perched so magnificently on top of the cliff, overlooking the Nile. Oh the mystery of it all. It would have been so very colonial and only for the aristocratic and the wealthy as there were many remnants of this staring back at us as we wandered our way through. Chandeliers, antiques galore and butlers dressed in

full attire making sure your every wish was attended to as you sat in the saloon room having tea and scones or maybe something a little stronger. It was the perfect place to ensconce oneself and write. What luxury! I imagined how, over the months, the other guests and their characters had been easily entwined into her famous mystery murder novel. Such great inspiration would have been ignited as she sat in her suite with stunning views and wrote morning and night. We stopped for light refreshments at one of the restaurants overlooking the Nile. Sinking into the comfy chairs we could have happily stayed there for a night or two. Alas, it was time to board our luxury cruise boat and commence our adventure on the Nile itself.

In many lives there are many masters...

Some would say I had the "life of Riley" and looking around me right at this minute they wouldn't be far off being right! How lucky was I? Here I was, on board a beautiful cruise boat, cruising down the Nile being spoilt rotten with every need at hand, waiters at my beck and call and sunbathing by the pool after a wonderful day of sightseeing at the ports of Kom Ombo and Edfu, where Walid shared more Egyptian history with us. Pure magic. I was having a few moments of my own time to relax, close my eyes and drift off into what I called, never-never land. Soaking up the last of the sun's rays and looking out to the banks of the Nile it felt like I was in biblical times. There was a lone Egyptian man with his clay pot collecting water and his trusty donkey close by, a felucca in the distance floating slowly along the Nile and the lush green foliage, dense in parts, lining the banks. Such simplicity and beauty all rolled into one. It was enhanced by the slow motion movement of the ship and it was as if everything was on a go slow, not like the fast paced cities we live in these days. What a great way to holiday!

Dragging myself from the deck lounger, not wanting to move I was so comfortable, I quickly got myself back to my cabin and ready for an experimental session with the rest of the group. Amongst the group there were some very gifted healers and we had decided to share our gifts and practice our healing work in the high vibrational energy of Egypt. Nothing had prepared me for what happened next. All 12 of us were packed into the cabin with little standing room left. Christine was the lucky first lying on the bed and the rest of us standing in a circle around her. Everyone had placed their healing hands either on Christine or just above her in what we know as the auric field and with eyes closed and healing being sent, Christine was being led through a regression.

Before long, she was back in another life and one that was not so fortuitous. The tears began rolling down her cheeks as she explained what she was seeing in the life she had been regressed back to. She was very poor and on her own with her small children that she was fending for. With no money to buy food she had stolen a mere loaf of bread and some fruit from a wealthy trader and had been caught. Her punishment was to be hung. With the tears now uncontrollably pouring down her face she began to describe in great depth the scene ahead of her and the deep sense of grief and guilt she felt for her children. It was so real for me, not only because of the sadness and pain that I could feel Christine was experiencing but something strange was happening. My throat was becoming tighter and tighter and I was having trouble swallowing. What was I to do? I was beginning to panic but did not want to bring any

attention my way. Would I be able to breathe properly any time soon? I realised that I was being given the gift of experiencing the past life of the person being regressed in my actual physical body. It was very bizarre, especially not being able to say anything as everyone else was working with the healing energy and participating in the regression. Christine continued to describe how the rope was being put around her neck as she was raised up and dispensed with in midair for those last few moments. Then the feeling of the rope becoming tighter and tighter before it was released and she took her last breath.

Knowing I had to leave the room, I urgently headed out into the corridor to gasp large quantities of air as I was trying to comprehend what had just happened. Wow, how amazing! What an incredible lesson for us all, acknowledging the power of what we cannot see, the power of energy especially in a high vibration, the significance of past lives and the direct connection to our current life. As well as how our soul records and stores the memories for us to remember at the precise time it is needed to heal or strengthen a behaviour, thought pattern or belief. Everyone left a little overawed and somber at the same time with their minds racing and reviewing what had just happened as we hurriedly got ready for another fun filled night on board the boat, then a few hours sleep before being up and at it the next day.

Our cruise ship was still moored in Luxor and we had risen very early hoping to avoid the hordes of tourists that would be visiting the Valley of the Kings and the Valley of the Queens. We were hoping to be some of the first to arrive for the day and explore this very important part of Egyptian history. On board our coach and driving to the west bank of the Nile to a point located opposite the necropolis of the ancient city of Thebes located on the east bank, Walid was sparing nothing as he took us on yet another visual journey. He was explaining how the moment a Pharoah was born a very important mission was to be carried out and that was to find the perfect place for the Pharoah to be buried. The Egyptians believed that after they died, their "Ka" (life source, essence and soul) would continue to live in the afterlife as it had been living within them during their life on earth. They believed the "Ka" of the individual needed a body to return to and that is why they mummified their dead. There was great emphasis put on the level of wealth that a Pharoah had in this life and being able to take that with him or her into the afterlife to continue with all of the same privileges, activities and social hierarchy. Many of the tombs were found to have contained painted murals, food, statues and other treasures. To be accepted into the afterlife, the Pharoah would have to navigate his or her way through the underworld and make their way to the Hall of Final Judgement. This is where they stood before the 42 divine judges and pleaded their innocence of any wrong doing in this life. They then had their heart weighed, as this contained a record of all of their actions in this life, against the feather of the goddess, Maa't that represented truth and justice. If their heart was lighter, then they had a clear passage through to the afterlife.

We all agreed that it was fascinating to learn about the strong Egyptian beliefs, sacred ways and mythology in which a human entered and departed this world. Arriving at the Valley of the Kings we were given a set of headphones and began to make our way into a selection of the tombs. Soaking up the history and stepping further into the depth of the

tomb we were mesmerised by the hieroglyphics, original artwork and the grand sarcophagus located at the end of the tomb. It must have taken years and an army of men to construct these tombs. King Tutankhamen's tomb was the highlight of our visit with much chatter and discussion about it in the coach as we headed back to Karnak where we were to spend the remainder of the afternoon.

Trust and you shall receive…

Closing my eyes and drifting in and out of sleep with the motion of the bus, all of a sudden I found myself being given information! I was being told by the way of words in my mind that there was a message for Walid, our tour guide. What? I thought, is this for real? I was being shown visions of the Statue of Liberty in New York and told that his uncle, who was a pilot with Egypt Air, was telling me that there was poisonous gas put into the air conditioning system on the aircraft. I did not know exactly what it meant but I kept listening. I was then told certain information about his uncle's children and wife and that she was to remarry and he approved of the new husband to be. Then I was told that Walid must wear the "ring" and that he must follow his heart as his world would open up in front of him if he did so. What on earth was that all about? How could it be that my third eye and psychic connection was becoming stronger and stronger while travelling Egypt? It was such a powerful message leaving me a little dumb-founded. Even so I pulled my notebook out and began writing everything down, making sure not to miss a thing. Was I to tell Walid this? No, surely not, I cannot do that or he might think I have lost the plot! Still, I knew very confidently within myself that this information was not made up and there was a significant reason for it being passed on to me so that I could pass it on to Walid. Tucking the notes away in my bag I convinced myself that I would certainly not be sharing this information just yet but maybe there would be a time that would be right. Floating off again into a deep relaxed state I drifted in and out of sleep on the bus.

Once met never forgotten.....

Bang, I jolted forward and woke myself up out of my dream state to find that the others were beginning to disembark from the coach to visit my favourite jewellery store. I wondered if the beautiful old man was still there, the one who made my last visit to this area so very special. I hoped so. Sure enough, there he was, perched up on his seat overseeing the place. I gave him a big smile and headed towards him to say hello. He saw me coming and welcomed me with open arms along with a gorgeous smile that he could not wipe off his face. Taking my hand he kissed my palm as only a charming Egyptian man can do and promptly said to me, "Welcome home my queen." I felt a little embarrassed, what did he mean by this? Grabbing my arm he guided me to a counter and began to pull out some stunning pieces of jewellery. There was one in particular; a delicate ring made of gold in the shape of the famous Egyptian ankh. He proceeded to put it on my middle left hand finger and tell me that it was connected directly to my heart. Wow, it did not matter that he spoke pigeon English, he certainly had a way of making an impact on me. Knowing that the ankh was the "key of life" and a symbol of eternity I felt very privileged to be wearing this representation of such ancient wisdom. Looking down at my newly acquired treasure he proceeded to tell me, "Know that my wings will always be at your

back guiding you on your journey and welcoming you home to Egypt whenever you can return." Looking him directly in the eyes I felt the tears well up inside of me remembering how the first time I had met him he had told me that I had been here before, not in this life but another. Shivers tingling throughout my body I wanted to slip out of the shop and digest what had just happened. Egypt and its magic had certainly cast its spell upon me once again.

It was that sad time once again where I had to depart from my beloved Egypt. On our last night back in Cairo we were sitting in the Sheraton Hotel with Walid, after a delicious last supper smoking the shisha pipe and reminiscing on all of the wonderful times we were so lucky to have had over the past couple of weeks.

Saying our last minute farewells to Walid before we retired for the night I had a flash thought. Now was the time to give Walid the piece of paper with the messages on it that I had been given about his uncle so I popped the folded piece of paper into his hand and said, take this home and read it and if you have any questions let me know.

It was not long before I heard from him. Upon checking my emails in Kuala Lumpur where I was stopping to break the journey en route back to New Zealand, I found an email from Walid. He proceeded to tell me that his uncle had been accused of committing a suicidal act and that the Americans had said he was responsible for taking Egypt Air flight 990 down in 1999 off the coast of New England, USA. He confirmed that his aunt was looking at remarrying but the most haunting confirmation was that of the ring. He told me that his mother and father's home had burnt down and when they went to see if there was anything that could be retrieved he took only one thing and that was his father's ring. To this day, Walid is contesting his uncle's innocence and rightly so.

Thank you my precious Egypt for your incredible high vibrational energy that allowed and encouraged my third eye to open up even further as I spent time back in this ancient land discovering and remembering more of myself.

CHAPTER FIVE:

Hopi and Navajo Initiation

CHAPTER FIVE:

Hopi and Navajo Initiation

Geronimo – this was the name my dad used to call me from as far back as I can remember. There was no explanation as to why he chose this name but for some reason, it stuck. It wasn't until many years later the connection and significance of the name would have an even greater impact as I stepped into intuitive healing work that stemmed from shamanism. Geronimo, the famous Apache India, was never a chief but a medicine man, a seer and a spiritual and intellectual giant. It was inevitable and no surprise that I found myself being drawn to Sedona and its strong native American presence with the Hopi and Navajo tribes. It was time to deepen my shamanic connection and there was no better way than going to the source itself.

Excitement was building as I had spent many hours preparing, to-ing and fro-ing with the Native American guide I had chosen to work with as we put together the itinerary for my group. Finally, I was taking my first spiritual tour to Sedona and as before, things were mysteriously falling into place.

Having spent hours researching and planning what I thought was the perfect itinerary I was not prepared for the phone call that came out of the blue. "Yes, that's right," I heard myself saying, "I have a tour departing shortly to Sedona, would you like to join us?" The woman on the end of the phone then proceeded to tell me that she had just returned from Sedona and that she would not recommend the guide I was using at all. My heart sank as I asked, "Why not?" She told me that he liked

the ladies too much and it had caused a problem in the group tour she had just been on with him. Oh no, what was I to do? We were leaving in about six weeks, I had a full group and they were all ladies. How seriously should I take this random phone call? Feeling sick inside, I decided to sleep on it and make a decision in the morning.

I was up at the crack of dawn and heading downstairs to the computer, my decision to explore other options swirling in my head, I felt confused and bewildered. I could not believe what I saw when I opened my computer. Sitting in my "inbox" was an email from another company in Sedona! No way. Was this a sign; was I meant to look no further and go with them? I had never heard from them before so how on earth did I get a copy of their newsletter on my computer and on this exact morning? Tapping away furiously I immediately sent an email to Sandra, the owner, to ask how she was placed to be my guide over the time that we were planning to be there and if so what sort of itinerary could she propose. Spirit was certainly guiding me and looking after me as this woman turned out to be not only available but super efficient and, as I was to see, extremely dedicated to the shamanic way of life and the Hopi and Navajo people.

The day of departure dawned and I was off on the next adventure. Arriving in Phoenix after many hours on aircrafts and at airports, the group gathered around as I signed my life away with the rental car papers. Hopping into the car, I made sure the GPS system was working and we managed to navigate our way out of Phoenix and onto the highway heading towards Sedona. Everyone was tired but too excited to sleep. The further we drove the more barren it became. Its beauty was extremely striking. We were waiting for that moment when we turned the corner and would see the famous red rocks of Sedona for the first time. It was not long before we did just that. Nothing prepared us for the breathtaking magnificence of the vast red rock mountains spread out before us. The sun was starting to fall and the soft hue reflecting on the mountains shone brightly back at us deepening the colours even more. Feeling as if we had been welcomed with open arms to this special land we soaked up the pure magnitude of the different shapes and sizes that were endlessly displayed in front of us.

We were to meet Sandra our guide, in the parking lot outside the Frontier Health Food Store. While driving from Phoenix to Sedona I had noticed that one of my eyes was becoming rather sore, with an annoying itch and redness developing as it began to swell and puff up. What on earth was happening? With the healing work that I practiced I knew that this was not a random thing but was happening for a reason as my body had reacted so quickly. I wondered what I was contemplating at a subconscious level. It then dawned upon me that I was nervous about bumping into the guide that I had originally communicated with as I had confirmed working with him and then I had let him down at the last minute. It had been unavoidable but still, I did not like having to do that. Sure enough, whether it was Murphy's-Law or a sixth sense or some negative energy at play, but who was the first person I saw when we pulled up into the parking lot? That's right, it was the guide! I could not believe it. Was my eye reacting in this way because, "I did not want to be seen?" I tried to keep my voice soft as we all piled out of the car and headed towards the store hoping like heck that he did not hear the different accents and realise that we were indeed a New Zealand/ Australia group. What a great start!

Introducing ourselves to Sandra we arranged to meet the next morning for our first adventure out on the land where she would lead us through a series of shamanic journeys with the drum. Ooooh, we couldn't wait! But, in the meantime, people needed to be fed and watered and there was much needed sleep to be had.

Journeying to the beat of the drum…

Up early and keen to explore the many vortex sites of Sedona we managed to fit in a walk along one of the trails of the famous Cathedral Rock site before we had to meet Sandra. Feeling energised and ready to adventure further, we headed out onto the land to learn from our guide as she took us through some powerful drumming journeys in preparation for the "real thing," whereby we would leave in a few days for the Hopi Mesas and Navajo land. In the meantime, our first journey was to connect with the juniper plant. This was a plant that was very sacred to the Native Americans with a multitude of uses. It was used as a tool for protection, healing, longevity plus purification and for some, such as the Hopi, it was also a clan symbol. What a powerful way to be initiated and connected to mother earth's energy here in Sedona and the presence of our Native American ancestors who were with us in spirit.

Clambering to find ourselves a comfortable spot on the soft sand-like soil, Sandra sat waiting, a rather foreboding figure, as she began to beat the drum in preparation for the journey. Her animal totem, she had told us, was "Bear" and when I looked at her in that moment I knew why. She was strong, commanding and very powerful, even a little frightening. Close your eyes Sharon and just let yourself go, you know you are in very safe hands. Even though she may be a little gruff, you know she has dedicated her life to this path and has spent many years practicing this work. She was a great teacher.

As the drumming became louder I found myself immediately being transported, travelling down through the roots of the juniper tree at breakneck speed into the heart of mother earth where the fire was burning. Who was that I could see sitting beside the fire? As I got closer I could see it was one of the elders waiting for me to sit with him. He was ready to share his wisdom so I seated myself down in awe of his presence and listened intently.

"Young one, let the fire within you ignite, let it shine. Draw on this flame and you will receive the energy of the juniper to help you on your path."

In the distance I could hear Sandra guiding us and asking us to retain the message and what we had seen or felt and bring it back with us as we travelled back up the roots of the juniper tree to where we were sitting in ceremony. Brought back with fast and loud drumming, we were all sitting looking at each other with slightly dazed looks on our faces. If this was the start of things to come we were going to learn much about ourselves as we journeyed deep within. Sandra then called us back into a circle and we began to share what we had experienced. Time just flew and before we knew it, it was time to head back into town and have lunch before we did a second journey that afternoon.

Having a few hours break to eat and explore we could not wait to get ourselves out to the shops. We had never seen anything like it. There was such an incredible array of metaphysical shops and health and wellbeing

practices. It was going to be heaven in this little slice of paradise for the next couple of days.

Oh where to start, upper or lower Sedona? Thank goodness we had a car that could transport us between the two as we were spoilt for choice. Laughing and chatting, everyone in the group was starting to relax and getting to know each other a little more.

As we connect with the shaman within we grow...

Back in the large transport van we headed over to Sandra's place where we would spend the afternoon sitting in the newly constructed medicine wheel in her garden for our second drumming session of the day. This time round we were going on a journey to meet the Shaman. Finding a comfortable spot in the garden with the trees sheltering us from the blazing heat we settled down once again to the hypnotic beat of the drum. In the distance, Sandra was leading us, guiding us over the red rocks towards a cave where we were to meet our Shaman guide. On our visionary journey we were asked to take note of any animals that were on the path. Ahead of me I saw wild horses and then a snake slithered across the path in front of me. Coming closer to the entrance of the cave we were encouraged to enter it, even though it looked a little frightening, I stepped into the darkness, putting one foot in front of the other. Ahead in the distance, a ray of natural light was shining in at the back of the cave and there was a beautiful Native American Shaman waiting patiently for me with a gift. I took myself closer to him and he passed me the most stunning large black stone. Thanking him for his gift and spending time conversing telepathically I heard the drum beat getting louder and louder as Sandra reminded us it was now time to say our goodbyes and follow the path that we had taken back to the here and now, where we were sitting in her garden. It had felt so real. Did I know the Shaman that I had seen in my journey? Writing notes in our journals and discussing the symbolic representation of the animals, I discovered that the horse represented strength and support to carry me through. The snake represented transformation plus the shedding of an old skin so the new could come through as well as snake medicine, which is so very powerful. I knew without a doubt that further into the trip there would be synchronicities relating back to these messages.

Sandra seemed very pleased. She had connected us to the juniper plant and its cleansing properties had assisted in our purification so we could step into a higher vibration as we ventured onto the Hopi Mesas, traditional pueblo villages located on the Colorado plateau and private Navajo land in Canyon de Chelly. We had all met our shaman guides individually and our animal totems had revealed themselves. We were ready for the earth medicine retreat and all that we would be exposed to for our higher learning over the next week.

In asking permission from the ancestors we are respected…

Breakfast under our belt and bags packed, today was the day we were heading out of Sedona on the long awaited trip to the Hopi Mesas where there were still three of the oldest continually inhabited villages in North America. Leaving Sedona behind, we began the climb through Oak Creek Canyon towards Flagstaff. With steep canyon walls, a roaring

river and dense foliage on both sides it was absolutely spectacular. Taking it slowly around the intensely sharp bends I wondered how on earth people could drive on a road like this with huge campervans towing either their own jeep or boat behind them! Craziness I thought, even for an adventurous Kiwi!! Winding our way up and up and up we eventually reached the edge of the Colorado plateau. I knew it was about now that I was supposed to communicate with my ancestors in spirit, asking them for permission to travel across their lands on this spiritual journey. I had been taught that it was the protocol, to have respect for the ancestors that had walked the land before us. As we ventured further onto the Mesas I could not help but think that it looked so much like Tibet in parts. It was extremely barren and volcanic. Could they have been joined together many thousands of years ago? I found out later that this area was also known as the Mongolian plateau so maybe some truth rang in this thought after all. Further into the trip I also noted how similar the Hopi and Navajo were to the Tibetans. If only the land could speak!

We were in luck as it turned out that one of the mesas was being used for a ceremony so Sandra managed to get permission to take us right into the thick of things. Parking the car and then walking past the traditional adobe houses into the heart of the village we had to make our way past many of the locals dressed in traditional costume and those fighting for a good viewing point to see the dancing. Next thing we were climbing up stairs and standing on the rooftops overlooking the village square, rubbing shoulders with the locals and joining in the festivities. You could see that this was an important day, one of tradition and celebration. It was an honour to be here amongst it all. Next up was the water maiden dance and to follow was the basket-throwing dance. It was a hive of activity with bursts of colour everywhere as young and old waited their turn to dance and participate in the age-old traditions. Rohanna, our beautiful Hopi guide, had met us here at the village and was now beckoning for us to follow her as we headed to the next mesa where her home was located. We were going to meet her family and share a meal with them. Lewis, her husband, was waiting for us along with her daughter, son and grandchildren. Welcomed warmly into the home we all squeezed in and sat around the dining table where large pots of tortilla chips, beans and corn bread awaited us. It was simple fare delivered with love.

We learnt that Rohanna was an important member within the community and led the sacred woman's ceremonies and Lewis had his role as well, practicing snake medicine and other rituals in the kiva – an underground circular room that was used for spiritual ceremonies. Lewis was also an accomplished carver and highly respected for the Hopi kachina dolls he made for the village. Watching him at work as he carved the intricate shapes into the soft wood, some of them having just been painted and drying, we began to understand the depth of tradition that was still being practised. Great importance is given to the "kachinas" as they are spirits or personifications of things in the real world. The Hopi believe that they represent the spiritual beings themselves and they use the kachina dolls to educate their children in the ways of life, with their representation of nature and historical events and their bridging or connection to the fifth world – the Taalawsohu. Before long, we had Lewis displaying his collection of dolls and the group negotiating on price as a lucky few made precious purchases.

Most of the village lived below the original mesa itself. After lunch we decided to take a walk before the long drive through to Chinle, which is where we were to stay for the night before heading into Canyon de Chelly to spend time on Navajo land in retreat. It was fascinating to see how the Hopi had positioned their villages on the highest points of this barren, stark, volcanic plateau so that they had a 360 degree view of the valley and beyond. Once again I pondered on how painstaking it must have been to climb to this point every day as they constructed the adobe buildings that became their fortresses.

It was with a few tears and fond farewells to Lewis and the family, having felt like we had known them forever, that we hit the road again. Luckily for us, Rohanna was coming so that she could share her wisdom and teachings over the next few days. Everyone loved her, such a warm heart, beautiful smile, great sense of humour and a deep spiritual knowledge of the Hopi and their traditions. It was obvious her that life had not been easy but this did not seem to stop her vibrant spirit. We were beginning to realise that we were in for some very special days ahead.

Driving across the plateau at high speed, as Sandra used to be a heavy truck driver and knew the road well, there were some close calls but we were in safe hands. Stopping en route to see some of the famous rock art in the middle of nowhere and a trading post for the compulsory loo stop, we made it to Chinle in good time. Stories were being shared and there was an undercurrent of both excitement and nerves as everyone knew that tomorrow was the start of something rather magical. We were to head into the heart of Canyon de Chelly and camp for three nights on private Navajo land with Sandra, Rohanna and Daniel our Navajo guide whom we had not met yet. So it was best that we get an early night and a comfortable one in before we had to sleep on bedrolls, or should I say mother earth, for the next three nights! Lights off and those last few words whispered with my roommate as I drifted off into the dreamtime. Next thing I knew it was morning again as the last remnants of sunrise were apparent through the windows.

Releasing my Pain, I Heal…

Hopping into the shower as I was thinking about what we were heading to, or trying to imagine, I became aware of a dull pain on my hips. I looked down and saw to my surprise that I had a rather angry rash on both of them. This stopped me in my tracks as I wondered if it had anything to do with the sweat lodge that we were going to participate in a little later on that morning. With no time to worry it was out of the shower, bags packed and down to the parking lot to meet Daniel, our Navajo guide.

There he was, larger than life with his long black hair flowing freely down his back, a little overweight, with a wide face that seemed serious, until he broke into a cheeky grin, hinting that he was going to be great fun. Sure enough, before long he was cracking the jokes and looking sideways at Sandra to make sure he wasn't going to get into trouble. Ha, ha, ha, we loved him and it didn't take us long to realise that he was a bit of a rebel and a trickster. Rohanna and he seemed to have a special connection and looking at them it was wonderful to see, the Hopi and Navajo, round faced and chiselled face, soft and gentle, strong

and defiant but no matter what, a bond indeed. Piling us all into the open jeep, Daniel was enjoying having the girls sitting so close to him and he was teasing them about the bumps to come and warning them to watch out for the handbrake. With lots of laughter and shrieks we began the bumpy ride into the canyon up and down sand banks, holding on for dear life and wishing for it to end as soon as possible.

Finally, the terrain seemed to flatten out and we were allowed to get out and walk part of the way. For the first time, I was truly able to take in my surroundings. Known as the 'womb," Canyon de Chelly was an absolutely spectacular natural formation. Here I was, standing deep within the canyon on the valley floor, feeling as though I was hidden from the world and wrapped between two extremely high red rocked canyon walls. Awesome! It was so powerful that words could not express the sense of wholeness I was feeling at that moment.

With clear blue skies, the sun beating down and not a cloud to be seen we approached Daniel's land. It was just beautiful with lush vegetation in patches, a small adobe hut called a hogan that he had been building for himself and the most important place, the campfire, the meeting place. Sandra was already there setting up her food supplies and unloading the van with our tents and bedding. Handing out orders she gave us our first job – to find a spot to set up our tents. Then when that was done it would be coffee time around the campfire before we headed off to participate in our first ever sweat lodge. Nerves were running at an all time high.

Changing into our swimwear, we walked as a group across the land to where Daniel was waiting for us in front of the fire that had been burning, since the wee hours of the morning, to heat the stones. There he stood, outside the traditional sweat lodge with his eagle feather in one hand and a serious look on his face. This was not the time for jokes. Everyone stepped in line and one by one we stood in front of the fire as Daniel smudged us with his eagle feather and the smoke from the juniper branches he had been burning. This was being done to cleanse and purify us before we entered the sacred space of the sweat lodge. Daniel explained that there would be four rounds and at the end of each round there would be extra hot stones placed in the middle of the sweat lodge to increase the heat. Once inside the sweat lodge you had the chance to communicate with the spirit of the four directions and their animal totems, grandfather sky, mother earth and Great Spirit itself. The purpose of this age old ceremony was to enter the space one way and as you communed with the spirit you would get the chance to release your negative thoughts, patterns, worries and sadness so that you exited with a new frame of mind, feeling lighter, cleansed and in fact symbolically reborn.

Entering on our knees, one at a time, we all managed to squeeze into the teepee completing the circle with the hot stones in the centre and Daniel seated with his back to the entrance. My knees touching the persons alongside of me, my head touching the top of the teepee, I got myself in as comfortable a position as possible. Already feeling the shortness of breath I was wondering how on earth I was going to cope with four rounds! Maybe the tip I had been given whereby I was to put my head as close to the earth as possible and to try and get a little more air by lifting up the tent flaps behind me might come in handy. Time stood still as Daniel began to call in the four directions and their animal totems,

the Eagle of the east, the Coyote of the south, the Bear in the west and the Great White Buffalo of the north. As Daniel communed out loud with Great Spirit he brought up different topics to discuss but that were relevant to us all. He was the elder leading the ceremony and when he finished speaking we could either add to the topic at hand or pass as it went around the circle to his left. With the first round completed more stones were being placed upon the pile already smoldering in the centre and those who needed to were allowed outside for a few minutes to cool down. Being brave, I stayed where I was, deep in thought, sweat starting to trickle down my body. Second round and everyone was back in place and Daniel was already deep in conversation with the animal spirits, mother earth, the ancestors, nature divas and Great Spirit. Then something quite incredible happened. The skies opened up and I heard thunder and then the rain began to fall. How amazing, considering it had been blue skies and sunny all day. In this moment it was crystal clear to me how deep the connection was between Spirit – the gods and nature, in other words, heaven and earth. It was as if the spirit of rain was hearing our prayers and washing us with her tears for further cleansing.

With the sound of the rain hitting the teepee and the rolling thunder in the distance I was bought back to the present as the conversation was being passed around the circle.

The second round was completed and round three was commencing. My legs were getting a little sore but I took another few deep breaths focusing back in on the conversation and sharing what was happening within the circle. Then it hit me. I could not stop it, this deep welling brewing up inside of me. It was my turn in the circle and a sharp guttural sound escaped from my mouth before I had a chance to repress it and tears began to fall down my face. Then the words followed. I found myself saying, that I really wanted to release the sadness that was consuming me and that I was holding onto for missing out on the opportunity to have children in this life. I knew I had been sad about this but to feel it at this depth and rising up without any foreknowledge was truly a cathartic moment for me. Exhausted after my outburst, the remainder of the ceremony was a blur.

Sitting back at the campfire, coffee mug in hand, bathing in my own thoughts I had a revelation. Oh my goodness! This morning I had woken to find a rash on my hips. Could it be that it was my physical body preparing to release the hurt that I carried? It was exactly where it should have been, if we think of the saying child bearing hips!! It was truly a life changing moment for me, such deep healing.

After such a big experience we were given some free time to just rest, eat, write in our journals or start making our prayer ties which we would need for our vision quest tomorrow night. Later this afternoon we were to commence a drumming journey to meet our guides before we finished the day with a medicine wheel ceremony. There was no doubt that I would sleep like a baby, even on the rock hard ground!!!

Closing our eyes and sitting in a circle, the familiar beat of the drum seemed even louder as it echoed off the canyon walls. Down we went into a deep meditative state with Sandra guiding us in the distance. I was excited to meet a new guide, and I wondered who it would be. Then out of nowhere, there he was, a young Native American Indian man, with his feet firmly on the ground staring me straight in the face. I

introduced myself and he returned the greeting by letting me know his name, Crimson Rain. He told me he was with me to give me strength when I needed it and to call on his energy whenever I wanted to. Slowly returning to the campfire with the beat of the drum having connected naturally with the beat of my heart, I found myself thinking about the first ever guide I was introduced to, "Singing Rain, Navajo" and now it seemed that I had another ancestor from the rainmaker family who was with me in spirit. Wow, my heart was singing.

What a huge day and it wasn't even over yet!! In the distance I could see Rohanna and Sandra pulling the weeds away from the medicine wheel that was hidden under the overgrown foliage. Calling us over and asking us to bring ourselves, the drums, rattles and blankets we made our way with great anticipation. Having had Rohanna share the history of the medicine wheel and its importance, especially from a healing perspective, we knew that what we were about to participate in would be deeply profound.

Entering the wheel from the East, the direction of spring and new beginnings we all walked in a clockwise direction until we were stationed at one of the four directions and then Rohanna began to chant in her native tongue calling in the ancestors and all of those in spirit who were to be with us today. Feeling shivers down my spine and tears at the corner of my eyes, I stood still and held myself together. Sandra then moved around the wheel calling in each of the animal totems, the energy associated with them and the spirit of each direction as well. The energy was so powerful, connecting us at a deep soul level. Each of us took a few moments to enter the centre of the wheel to speak out loud with Great Spirit, asking for what it was we wished to have healed. It was a very personal moment, one that did not seem to matter as we knew that the people we were in the wheel with were part of our soul family and there would be no judgement. We were all on the same journey of learning to trust and wanting to release some of those heavy burdens we had carried with us for far too long.

Having chosen earlier, which part of the wheel I was to lie in when each of us would have our individual healing moment, I found myself being wrapped in blankets, totally cocooned as if I was in my mother's womb. With the eagle feather that Rohanna had given me clutched tightly to my chest all that was exposed now was my face. I felt so very safe. Haunting native words echoed above me as Rohanna began her chanting and then, the beat of the drum, the shake of a rattle and the distant sound of the rain stick joining in. Eyes closed and I began to journey deeper and deeper as the instruments came closer, almost too close, deafening almost, and then they would fade away. There were many visions, many messages and the deepest sense of being at one with the cosmos. How long I was there I do not know but I did not want it to end. Every cell in my body had been awakened and I knew that deep healing was occurring. Next thing I was being unwrapped and helped slowly up so that I was steady on my feet and guided to a chair to sit down and let it all sink in even further. After everyone had had their turn to be drummed and taken on their journey we closed the wheel and headed back to the campfire to keep ourselves warm and share our experiences.

With two incredibly healing experiences at such a deep level in one day I was shattered to the bones, but I felt immense gratitude. Sleeping

out in a canyon where there were plenty of wild animals would be a challenge. At least tonight we had tents to cover us, an outdoor loo close by and the burning embers of a campfire to keep us warm. It would be a different story tomorrow night!

Facing my Fear, I Receive…

Waking up, I realised that I was still alive. Thank goodness! Apart from a slightly stiff neck after a night trying to sleep on the ground I wasn't feeling too bad! Promising to be another gorgeous day the sun was starting to rise, the air was crisp and it was breakfast time. Pouring myself a coffee I sat talking to Daniel as the others crawled out of their tents, one after the other, to join us. Sitting around the campfire, Daniel was teaching us a game where I think he was being more entertained than we were! He was getting us to draw a river, a house, trees, a sun and a snake. After we had completed our drawings he then proceeded to tell us that the river represented the flow of life, the house represented how you saw your home, the trees represented your relationship to your mother and the sun to your father and last but not least the snake represented your sex life. There was great hilarity over a couple of the girl's pictures as their snakes were coiled up into tight balls. All joking aside, it is the most fascinating exercise, revealing how you view life and your relationships. I wondered if it was an old Navajo teaching or if it was Daniel making up his own version.

It was time to stop playing and get a little more serious as we sat around the campfire and waited for Daniel to share one of his precious Navajo gifts, the intricate art of sand painting. In Navajo tradition, the medicine man is called upon to paint for healing purposes only. The ceremony takes place in the heart of the hogan (traditional home of the Navajo) where the medicine man paints loosely on the ground while he is in his meditative state, chanting and communing with spirits, calling upon them to send their powers into the painting to help heal the patient. We were all totally mesmerised as Daniel sat crouched on his knees and the most beautiful drawing began to appear out of thin air. He was deftly picking up one coloured sand pile after another and allowing the sand to fall softly through his hands with such precision and speed. Not a word was uttered as he painted the finishing touches on the kachina figure allowing the medicine to be felt by us all.

It was a good thing that Daniel had chosen to use his medicine skills and demonstrate the sand painting ceremony to us because below the surface much had been brewing since the early hours of the morning. The wind had been picking up and it looked like a massive storm might sweep through the valley with the possibility of heavy rains as well. It was only a few months since the devastating floods in New Orleans and the locals were on high alert. Heated discussions were had between Sandra, Rohanna and Daniel. They were trying to keep them from the group but eventually they called me over to consult and hear my opinion on behalf of the group. In the meantime, one of the ladies had woken with a severe migraine and this was causing concern as well. Daniel and Rohanna were all for packing up and leaving the canyon while we could but Sandra was holding her ground. No, she did not want to, we were to stay and do the vision quest. She said we must trust the universe and that it would not be as bad as "fear" was allowing us to think it might be.

Ultimately, it came down to me. Did I want to take the risk and stay with my group or not? One of the mottos that I had always practiced within my travel company and with my people was that the majority vote won. Wanting to share with my people so that they did not feel dictated to but instead involved in the decision making, I decided to apply this with my group. I could have easily made the decision but from past experience, I knew when the team or the group made it, they owned it and it worked. All but one wanted to stay. They were prepared to take the risk. There it was, the majority vote won. We were staying.

The atmosphere was tense as we went about packing up our tents and loading them into the van in readiness for our departure the following day. Tonight we were to do our vision quest and sleep out on the land with no protection at all!!! We were scared and no wonder some of the group were experiencing migraines and finding themselves with a short fuse as they tried to prepare themselves mentally for the unknown ahead. Sitting around the campfire, the mood was sombre with most of us deep in thought as we put the finishing touches to our prayer flags. These were a really important item that we would be taking with us to help in creating our sacred circle that we were to sleep in overnight. Sandra was watching all of the time and offering her words of wisdom in her unique way. She was staunch and strong with not a lot of compassion to share at surface level and this was making some in the group even more concerned. Can't she see that we are shit scared? I heard one of the ladies saying to another. Of course she could, but it was her job to make us all feel like we could do this, to dig deep and pull on our survival instincts and inner strength. No use pussy footing around here, we were to draw on the Navajo warrior energy!

Having had lunch after completing a soul-retrieval drumming journey, Sandra was preparing us with our last minute tips before we were to head out onto the land to build our sacred circle. Thank goodness Sandra's hunch had been right as the bad weather had passed over us. We had chosen our individual spots the day before and the rules were that we were not allowed to see anyone else from our chosen piece of land as this would defeat the purpose of our vision quest. We needed to be totally and utterly alone - at least for as far as our human eye could see. It was comforting to know that over the ridge was the camp and Daniel, Rohanna and Sandra would be there if something untoward eventuated. Why was it so scary? Because of the wild animals that we knew lurked in the shadows of the canyon as well as the fact that we were sleeping under the stars on our own! It was an amazing test of courage, how to walk through fear and have faith all at the same time.

With my sleeping bag under my arm, my bag of snacks, journal, pen and torch I heard myself saying goodbye to the others. Wishing them luck and encouraging them with a greater confidence than I felt, my heart was beating and there were butterflies in my stomach. Turning and walking our separate ways was a rather surreal feeling. Here we were, on our own with only our thoughts and time on our hands for the next 20 odd hours. Arriving at my spot I began to make my sacred circle with the stones I could find on the ground all of the time communing with Spirit asking for protection while I set my intention as to what I wanted to gain out of stepping into my circle and this vision quest. Starting from the east, I placed my prayer ties in the four directions as I enjoyed the ceremony of this age-old Native American tradition. I had been so busy creating my circle and making sure I got it right that I had not

noticed the sun had begun to slowly set. Seeing things with more clarity and a much greater depth, the scene was truly magnificent, with the softness of the setting sun picking up different shapes and shades that were hiding in the canyon walls. I happily plonked myself down for a short rest on a large stone close by for a few moments breathing it all in.

It was time to say my prayers as I prepared myself to step into my sacred circle where I would spend as much time as possible, apart from the compulsory bathroom breaks. Standing at the edge of the circle, I looked up to the setting sun, opened my arms wide and called upon the Great Spirit, my spirit guides and those from the highest of realms to stand beside me guiding and supporting me as darkness approached. I stepped into my circle and made myself comfortable snuggling up inside my sleeping bag, journal alongside me and pen in hand. Finally, after all of the activity, as I lay down looking at the cloud formations I saw what looked like the head of an Indian chief with all of his headgear intact. Wow! The canyon walls had many nooks and crannies that I had not taken much notice of before. Having been taught how to detect a portal gateway to another realm within the rock face I was intrigued with what I was seeing for the first time and before I knew it, darkness was almost upon me. With a great sense of peace and trust waving over me, feeling totally connected to nature and mother earth herself, my fear of being out here on my own was subsiding. In fact, I was starting to enjoy it! The whole idea was to stay awake for as long as you could so that you could communicate with spirit, listening to the thoughts and ideas that weaved their way through your mind, taking notes whenever you felt it necessary. If you fell asleep, that was ok too, as travelling deep into the dreamtime allowed you to spin even more magic because when you awoke you had to listen intently to the messages that were being given and take note of the pictures you may have seen.

There were noises and they were unknown but every time I heard something I just said another prayer and visualised my sacred circle having glass walls that nothing could penetrate. The noise would eventually fade away and my heartbeat would make its way back to normal again. This time round, I had fallen into a deep sleep, waking to look up and, I swear, right in front of my eyes way up in the sky was something I had never seen before. There she lay, on a bench way up in the sky, a beautiful woman with the longest, darkest hair I had ever seen, dressed in a flowing white gown. I was told she was the moon goddess. Was I still dreaming or was this real or maybe it was what some would call a vivid imagination. It was in fact a full moon this particular night and the silver light of the moon made everything that much clearer. After jotting down some notes I found myself drifting back into the dreamtime even faster this time round. How much later I do not know, but waking up again I had very specific words I needed to write down in my journal….

> *"The earth's grid work has a large piece that has shifted. It is causing much dysfunction within the bionic movement, sort of like the shorting of an electrical circuit. Work is needed to rethread it back together. This has been caused by the severe abuse of mother nature to the extent that the layers have been erupted due to corrosion of the electromagnetic fields. Prayer and intent will work in reconstructing it. Please start with*

this and share it with whomever you can as the larger the intent and prayer the sooner this will be mended.

It can work very fast. Light years fast if you intend it to. Call on the gods to assist you, the whales and the anchors such as the pyramids, Pachamachac, Machu Picchu, the Tibetan Plateau, Stonehenge and Lake Titicaca. It is like a railway track where the track suddenly ends and there is nowhere for the current to go. Scientists are aware of the hole but they do not know how to mend it yet. As the electric currents build up with nowhere to go this causes much disaster. Explosion – then build up of currents for the air, for the ground, for the sky and this is one of the reasons for the many disasters that are occurring. Mother earth has been working so hard to hold the grid together. The stars have been assisting her as well but her strength is weakening. Respect and love of the land is needed to help heal this. Call on the ancient ones to share their advice and act on it."

Putting my pen down and letting out a long sigh, deeply connected with the cosmos, I found myself once again drifting back into the dreamtime. I was almost asleep and was woken to draw a picture of a snake and write the words, "snake knowledge – you must learn – study the medicine and use it in your work." Head back on the ground and there I went again, back into fairyland.

In and out of the dreamtime, waking, drawing and writing in a half sleep, half awake state it was not until the next day or many days later looking back through my journal that I realised just how important the messages had been for me. My subconscious mind, my soul had been speaking to me providing me with direction and specific teachings. It was just so incredibly powerful on so many levels.

This time around, in the wee hours of the morning, I woke with a start. What was that noise I could hear in the distance? It sounded like continuously rolling thunder. With my heart racing I scanned my immediate area and then out across the valley floor. By now it had become deafening as I realised it was a herd of wild horses. The sound of their hooves pounding on the dry valley floor echoing in the stillness of the canyon sent shivers down my spine. Expect the unexpected and learn to adapt at the speed of light with your surroundings and activities. Luckily for me they diverted their path and went alongside the camp on the other side of the canyon. Breathing back to normal I shone my torch to have a look at the time. It was 2 o'clock in the morning. Still a few hours to go before sunrise and safety!!

With the moon fading, the stars shining brightly and the darkness of the early hours still surrounding me I woke this time in a very deep dream state to see what looked like 40 or 50 men with long dark hair wearing nothing on their torsos and their backs towards me as they were walking through the canyon along the valley floor. It was obvious they were of Native American Indian decent. I wondered where they were going and what they were doing. Were they from a specific clan? It felt so real and I knew they were on a mission of some sort.

The next time I awoke the sun had begun to rise and I was ever so grateful to see the light, however the crispness in the air made me pull my sleeping bag tighter as I snuggled in, reflecting on the experience I had just had on my first vision quest. There were so many visions, so many entries in my journal and a great sense of accomplishment for having survived nature and the wildlife itself in the depths of the night. I wondered how the others had done. I could not wait to get back to camp and sit around the fire where we were to be treated with a special traditional Navajo pancake breakfast! Embracing the moment for a while longer I wrote a little more in my journal, took in the scenery one more time and then began to dismantle my circle thanking Great Spirit for looking over me during the night.

Back at camp there was much chatter as we all shared our experiences, the harrowing moments and the precious ones. Putting the finishing touches to our shields that were made with local willows and calf skin we painted any symbols or pictures we had been given during our time in our sacred circle. This was a fantastic souvenir to take home; let's just hope I could get it in through customs!

The last of our gear packed, we all piled into the jeep again as we said our goodbyes to the canyon and its womb like qualities that had nurtured us so beautifully over the past few days. It was time to head back to Sedona via one of the largest outpost stores where we could purchase any last minute souvenirs, then on to Rohanna's for another delicious meal with her family before we finally made it back to the city lights!

In the face of adversity, follow your heart…

Jewellery, paintings, smudge sticks, incense, eagle feathers, books, clothing, oh so many things to choose from. We could spend hours in the outpost store but Sandra was hurrying us up, "Come on guys we have a long drive ahead of us." At this moment I had just stepped into a room full of Kachina dolls and was observing them closely. One in particular had caught my eye so I had picked it up and was trying to work out the significance of this particular doll. Sandra came up behind me and told me it was known as the rainmaker but that all of the dolls in this store were machine made and it was much more authentic to try to purchase a hand carved one. So I reluctantly placed it back on the shelf and thought nothing more of it. We arrived at Rohanna's for lunch and Lewis was there to greet us with his large grin and cheeky ways. Asking him what he had been up to over the past few days he told us he had just finished carving a Kachina doll. He headed off to get it so that he could show off his latest creation. Returning to the room he proceeded to tell us it was a rainmaker Kachina. Well my jaw dropped and I did something I would never normally do. I butted in over and above my clients and said Lewis, I must have that, how much is it? Can I please purchase it off you! I then realised what I had done as I received a few not so pleasant glances from some of the group. I knew deep within me that I had to have it and if it meant that I would get into trouble I would have to take the risk.

With two significant spirit guides from the rainmaker family I felt it was talking to me and that it was essential for me to bring back the energy of the rainmaker Kachina to be with me when I practiced my

healing work. I hoped the group understood when I got a chance to explain. Having purchased a rain stick earlier on it felt like my supply of tools for practicing my shamanic healing were about to be complete. I loved it. Mainly crimson in colour I then realised that here was another synchronistic connection as my guide, that I had been introduced to on this trip, was crimson rain! She held a globe of the world in her hands, leaving no doubt in my mind that this represented to me the spiritual tours I was so passionate about. I'd found my Kachina doll.

The power of spirit...

Back in Sedona we had a few days left before it was time to leave so everyone was up early and ready to maximise the days. This morning we were heading out onto the red rocks to do an intuitive art class with the gorgeous Nataya of Sedona. Stumbling across this extremely talented lady I was excited for the group. Her bright, bubbly and compassionate personality was a nice contrast to working with our other guides where the tone had been quite a bit more serious. She was a breath of fresh air and an inspiration. Over the next few hours we learnt how to trust our intuition as we painted with water colours. Everyone was amazed at what they were creating as they let the mind go and followed the flow of their heart and the paintbrush. However, what everyone was secretly waiting for was the opportunity to have a one on one session with Nataya. She had a very special gift where she could paint a picture for you and give you a psychic reading at the same time. The more she painted, the more she discovered and the more it came together. It was incredible how she knew what was happening in your life as it was reflected in the painting. I could not wait for my turn.

Finally, it was my turn and I was sitting there in awe, as Nataya was busy telling me that I was part of the rainmaker family!!!! She had no idea what had happened yesterday when I purchased the doll from Lewis, nor the fact that I had Singing Rain and Crimson Rain as guides who worked with me in my healing work. I was so happy to have had my hunch confirmed. Being part of the rainmaker clan was hugely important to me. Later on, I learnt via Sioux legend how the rainmakers played such an important part in aiding fear to be faced and released. I trusted that with the energy of the rainmakers ingrained within me, I would be able to help people with this when they came to see me.

Last minute shopping and it was spend, spend and more spending!! What else could I fit into my suitcase? Entering a beautiful crystal shop I wondered if there might be anything in there that would take my fancy. Not too big, just something small that I could squeeze in as a reminder of Sedona. Then, there it was, staring me in the face. A large black rainbow obsidian stone with the most intricate heart carved in the centre of it. My mind went straight back to the drumming journey where we were taken to meet the shaman. Mine had handed me a gift and it was a large black stone that looked exactly like the one sitting in the cabinet in front of me. This was too much of a coincidence! Needless to say, it was bought before you could say "Jack Sprat sat on a candlestick."

Stepping outside, the next store was beckoning and then there looked like an interesting art gallery a few doors down that I wanted to take a peek at. On entering the gallery in front of me, as large as life there it was, the absolute exact scene of what I had been shown in my vision quest. I walked closer, shaking my head in disbelief. The painting depicted 40

or 50 Native American men walking through a canyon with their backs to us. My eyes shifted to the title of the piece – "Star Gazers." Oh my goodness this just topped the whole journey off. Smiling from the inside out I was so very happy to have had all of these amazing experiences on the return to Hopi and Navajo lands. I had reconnected with my past at a deep cellular level and received not only my own personal healing, but also the gift of the healer, and a full tool box to share with the others on my return.

CHAPTER SIX: Incan Wisdom

CHAPTER SIX:

Incan Wisdom

Staring out of the aircraft window, there they were, the most magnificent snow capped mountains, the Andes, bold and strong with the city of Santiago, Chile, nestled contentedly at the base of them. En route to Peru with a one night stopover in Santiago, the group was on a high as we were that one step closer to our final destination. With plenty of laughter and excitement we were attempting to have a conversation between ourselves and our guide as we made our way to the hotel. After dropping our bags it was out onto the streets to explore and embrace the Latino way of life, which was definitely very much based around coffee and conversation! With plenty of cafes, cake shops and wine bars scattered throughout the city there was no shortage of places to immerse oneself into the local scene. Around every corner, the architecture would surprise you with its intricate beauty and attention to detail. It was a city full of history and was pleasant to wander around as it was mainly flat and very well laid out. Buskers and artists on the street added a real splash of colour. With the first items of shopping secured and tired feet we headed back to the hotel for a meal before crashing for the night in preparation for an early start the next day.

Waking with a start I wondered where I was. I felt very strange and then I remembered I was in Santiago in a hotel room, not my bed at home. I knew immediately it was one of "those dreams" and I was to keep my body absolutely still so that I could allow the dream to fully integrate, to collate itself into my conscious mind, and remember every detail of it. Recalling the dream, I watched it replay itself as I had that familiar

feeling of being right there, in the dream, recording it in my mind like a computer, hoping not to miss a thing. I was in what looked like the desert where the terrain was sandy, flat, dry and arid. In fact, it looked very similar to the Giza Plateau in Egypt. Next thing I saw a very large face constructed of old brick that was light brown in colour. The face was alive and moving from side to side. Its eyes were looking directly at me. I had no idea where it was or what the symbolism represented. By this stage I had learnt that I was often shown things a day or two before I arrived at a destination while on these special journeys. It would unfold, of that I was sure. Pulling myself slowly out of that groggy state I found myself in when I was in the midst of a powerful dream, I got up, showered, packed and was on the way to the airport.

Disembarking from the aircraft and taking ourselves through customs we entered the arrivals hall looking for a sign displaying Lifestyle Journeys. Willaru, our guide, was to be there to greet us and transfer us to our hotel in the Mira Flores area of Lima. There he was, this very wise looking Peruvian elder. With the most serene face that beamed of wisdom and knowing, he clasped his hands together in a prayer position, bowed his head slightly and welcomed us home. I could feel the tears welling up in the corners of my eyes and knew the others were feeling the same. Just standing next to this beautiful man you immediately felt the love that emanated from him. In that moment we knew that this was indeed going to be a very special journey. Guiding us through the throngs of people we made our way outside to our minibus, climbed in and began the drive to the hotel. Massive billboards, shining lights, loads of traffic and buses overflowing with locals, this was our greeting to Lima, as we wound our way through busy streets. It was quite incredible how the standard of living could change within moments just between the airport and the Mira Flores area where we were to stay. This area catered specifically for the tourists and the more affluent locals, having greater safety measures in place.

The following morning after breakfast, we were ready to commence our transformational journey. The first few days would be spent south of Lima at sea level visiting Pachamachac and Huacachina, an oasis village just outside Ica and Nazca. Before saying goodbye to the staff and our quaint little hotel that had been home for the night, I noted the modest standards of our accommodation. Willaru believed it was important not to focus too much on the material world when participating in a spiritual pilgrimage. It was all about valuing and appreciating everything in moderation. This was just one of the many lessons we were to learn along the way. As we piled into the minivan with spirits high we listened intently to Willaru introduce himself officially, sharing a little of his background. Born a Quechua Indian he had been raised in the traditional way in a small village high up in the Andes. By the time he was a young man he had begun his own spiritual quest practicing first as a shaman and then wishing to explore further he decided to travel deep into the Amazon jungle for six months with nothing but the clothes on his back and the intent to connect with the masters. He emerged with a vision to travel to Cusco as a Chasqui (messenger) for the Great White Brotherhood dedicating his life to sharing the messages that he received on esoteric truth pertaining to the transitional times in which we live. Over the next few weeks we would hear many of his stories about his time in the jungle and the amazing things that happened along the way, leading him to where he is today and his dedication to his work.

After finally reaching the outskirts of Lima we were travelling south on the open highway, adjacent to the ocean and heading towards the ancient archeological site of Pachamachac. It was such a contrast from the city we had just left behind. On the coastal side, there were seaside villages dotted here and there filled with whitewashed buildings that were surrounded by many tropical trees and flowers that looked so inviting.

On the inland side of the highway it could not have been more different. This was where the poor lived. Periodically, on the side of huge sand mountains, there were large shantytowns that were highly populated. They were fondly known as parachute towns because it was as if someone landed straight from above in the middle of nowhere, claimed a piece of land as theirs and then the shantytowns grew from there. It was extremely sad seeing the massive contrast of poverty and wealth in such close proximity.

Our initiation in patience and so much more....

Bang! What was that noise? It was coming from the back of the car. Pulling over to side of the highway, the driver hopped out to see what had happened and soon reported that we had blown the rear right-hand tyre. We began clambering out of the car in the middle of nowhere, with the searing heat beating down, to find that the spare tyre was bald and the jack wasn't working. Not the best of news! Oh no, this was certainly going to test the patience of the group. Would they buy into the fear of being stranded in what seemed like the desert with nothing in sight or would they have faith? It was my job now to keep everyone calm, including myself, and reassure them with the thought that things like this did seem to happen on these pilgrimages. It was like the spirit realm above was definitely testing us. It was a compulsory part of going on a spiritual pilgrimage, to learn to have more compassion and understanding, patience and faith. As the driver was hastily trying to organise a replacement on the phone I reminded the group that we were in a third world country and the locals were used to dealing with situations like this. The sooner we relaxed and looked at the situation as a 'spiritual test' whereby we were not to panic and draw on our strength in the trust that it would soon be sorted, the faster we would be back on the road. They were a great group and understood the lesson and before long, miraculously, the spare tyre was delivered, speedily changed by the driver and it was on to Pachamachac.

Approaching the site, I could not believe the similarities between the Giza Plateau in Egypt and what I was now feasting my eyes upon. Willaru was explaining that during the Lemurian civilisation it had once been a highly respected mystery school where if your daughter or son would be chosen to attend, it would have been a huge honour as they could have become a great King or Queen. The mystery schools were spiritual schools where a typical day entailed four hours spent on chores and the remaining hours were for spiritual practice and learning. It seems that now in this day and age, we certainly have it the wrong way around. We would be lucky if we dedicated even an hour a day to spiritual learning as the bulk of our day is spent at work hunching over those boxes called computers! After parking the car, we gathered together in a group as Willaru began to walk and lead us to the furthest point in the distance. Walking single file we climbed stairs passing ancient ruins that must have once been temples or large worshipping spaces. Everyone knew to retreat and enjoy the time to just be with their thoughts. On reaching the horizon, lo and behold, below us we could see the ocean and the coastline stretching for miles. Willaru gathered us together in a circle and officially began our tour with a ceremony to welcome us back home calling upon Spirit to acknowledge that we had made it. Feeling like we were back in Lemurian times and being initiated into the mystery school as new students, the importance and beauty of the moment was felt by everyone.

I get it, yes, it all makes sense now! An "Aha" moment! It was during our single file walk when deep in my own thoughts I had it confirmed to me that the face I had seen in my dream in Santiago two nights before, belonged here. I was being told:

> *"It was the sister/brother connection between Egypt and Peru and the same size as the Sphinx. Connected by energy lines, bionic chords and electromagnetic fields there is much work that is accomplished between these two sites. They hold many of the records that are accessed by the higher dimensions. They are entrance portals to the other dimensions."*

Learning not to doubt the information I was given but instead to record it and accept that I was indeed meant to have been shown or given the words as inevitably later on I would have it validated by way of conversation or reading it somewhere. The thing I absolutely loved was that my knowledge of history was zero, as I never studied history at college and neither did I read history books. So it was reassuring to me that whatever I was shown or told was not preconceived.

Back on the road again, with fingers crossed that we would have no other mechanical hold ups, everyone settled in for the remainder of the drive. Arriving at Huacachina and checking into our quaint hotel located on the edge of the oasis, we had time to swim and rest, or, for the energetic ones, to climb the massive sand dunes that surrounded us before we would take off in our buggies to watch the sunset high up on the dunes. What a neat place to lounge in for a couple of days, soaking up the fun atmosphere as you tried your hand at sand boarding or just chilling out and mixing with the many tourists that were here. Zooming across the dunes, balancing off the edge of a sand dune one minute and finding ourselves at the bottom the next. The shrieks were a great sign that everyone was having an adrenalin rush that would certainly require a nice wine or two at dinner to calm us down. If we made it back in one piece that was!!

I was not sure what caused it. Maybe it was the sun and dive bombing on the dunes, or the couple of glasses of wine the night before, but something told me it was none of those. Instead, it was a good dose of food poisoning. Having woken up with projectile vomiting and diarrhoea I was not feeling too happy with myself. Only day two of the tour and the tour leader was laid up flat on her back! Luckily for me, Willaru took over and spent the morning with the group having a Q & A session and by lunch time I was feeling better and able to join them on the afternoon visit to one of the most fascinating privately operated museums in Peru.

Had another humanity existed...

Doctor Cabreras Stone Museum held 20,000 extraordinary rocks intricately carved with great precision. There have been many theories as to how the rocks with the carvings came to be found in the desert surrounding Ica. To this day, no one has definite proof, however, it is believed that they may have been carved by an ancient civilisation. Walking into the museum I was blown away by the stones, so many different sizes and such specific details entailing astronomy, physics and medicine. I wondered if they were connected to the mysterious Nazca lines as well. Could it be that there had once lived an advanced super intelligent species responsible for all of this ancient history? We will never know but it was wonderful to hypothesise with the group, dissecting the endless possibilities from a scientific and spiritual point of view. Jumping back in the minibus we continued our journey from Ica to Nazca across the barren plateau land with its dark sand that once again reminded me of both the Mongolian plateau in Arizona and the Tibetan plateau in Tibet. I wondered if this advanced super intelligent race was still alive today in another realm that we could not see and if they spent their time teleporting themselves from one plateau to another. Reigning my imaginative mind and theories back into the here and now I switched into tour guide mode as we had just arrived at our hotel in Nazca for the night.

Secretly, I was pleased that I did not have to do the Nazca flight again. Having done it a few times before, it was not something I wanted to do again in a hurry. Not because I did not enjoy it but I remembered all too well the nauseous feeling I had to deal with when the pilot shouted, hey lady, hey lady to the left, to the left, the monkey, the monkey as he dipped the plane for us to see out of the left hand side of the aircraft. Just thinking about it made me feel sick! I wasn't going to tell the group, though, as this would make them afraid and they were all so excited to see the Nazca lines. The morning was perfect and for once we did not have to wait too long to be allocated a time slot. They were weighed, given the safety talk, handed a life jacket and led to their four-seater aircraft as I stood by, reassuring them it would be awesome! Twenty minutes later they were back on the ground and climbing out of the aircraft, some looking a little greener than others. I knew for sure it would be the topic of the day as they recalled the pilot's words and the amazing sight of the Nazca lines themselves. Now it was time to jump back in the minibus and start the massive sojourn through the Andes to the Sacred Valley where the Apus, the great spirits of the mountains, awaited us.

The road was not for the faint of heart with its sheer cliff drops, no barriers and wind gusts that were becoming stronger the higher we climbed. "Why had I chosen to do this?", I asked myself. Because hardly any tourists did it and I liked to take my tours off the beaten track, but more importantly, it helped immensely with adjusting the body to the climb in altitude. This way, it was a steady pace instead of flying from sea level to 3,400m above sea level in one fell swoop. Weaving our way deep into the Andes we spent all day travelling, stopping for lunch and then finally at Abancay, a very traditional Peruvian town, for the night. What a delight it was to see no other tourists in sight. The locals went about their business, not worrying about us at all. It was up to us to just blend in.

Onwards and upwards, climbing even higher we made our way across many mountainous passes until we eventually hit the valley floor leading to Cusco. The terrain had changed quite dramatically where there was plenty of green grass, majestic trees, field upon field of crops with villages nestled into the mountains and the locals going about their business. We were here, finally. Yahoo! Some of the members in the group had dull headaches and were concerned about altitude sickness. Willaru made it clear that if they were to have an attack of altitude sickness then it was to be seen as a cleansing. A few of the group were confused by this explanation and I did not blame them. In the world that we came from, this would be the last form of medical explanation given for such a condition. However, having experienced altitude sickness before, I could vouch for the fact that it was indeed a cleansing. I noted that when I was in a good headspace my body had no problems with the altitude, however I had been to Peru before carrying emotional burdens and I had been struck down with altitude sickness. Interesting, very interesting.

It was on this leg of the journey when I was sitting next to Willaru on the coach that something quite special happened. He often sat with his eyes closed, deep in meditation and we knew not to disturb him. Most of us had been drifting in and out of sleep as well with the motion of the bus. Waking up suddenly, he turned to me and said, "You should write a book about your travels." There was something about the way in which he had just spoken with such clarity and intensity, as if it was an absolute moment of truth. I knew he had been given clear directions in his meditation to pass this message on to me. Noting it in my mind, I sat with that message for many years until I find myself finally writing the book he had talked about so long ago!

Speeding across the valley floor and climbing once again, the countryside was being left behind as we began approaching a large city where everything was becoming denser. There were many churches, schools and public buildings not to mention the people. I could have watched the people all day as they dressed so colourfully, especially the women with an array of woollen garments, layer upon layer, to keep them warm, and then finished off with the famous bowler hats that they wore! Oh such a beautiful race with their silky black hair, chiseled features, dark eyes and proud stance. Winding down cobblestone streets we began to enter Cusco with our eyes glued to the windows. Shop upon shop of goodies to purchase, restaurants, bars, travel agencies, touts on the street selling their wares, market stalls set up on corners.

Oh my god! I loved this city. I would never tire of it. Wandering the streets and finding fresh bread in a tiny bakery, delving into an alley and discovering exquisite art, jewellery and clothing. I could spend days here immersing myself in the way of life. I loved watching the Quechua Indians that came into the markets from their remote villages to sell their produce. With their fresh vegetables, meat and all of the superfoods that are such a staple part of their diet, they had thriving businesses. These were the foods that the world had just begun to discover and had been going crazy about, and here they were in bulk supply, quinoa, macca, cacao, lucuma and many others. The group would love staying here for the next few nights and exploring this vibrant, ever-changing town to their heart's content.

We were having so much fun. During the day we would meet with Willaru and he would take us around the outskirts of Cusco visiting the sacred sites. There were often many other tourist groups and I found it fascinating to hear their guides talking to them from more of a conventional view about the Incan empire and the Spanish conquest. When Willaru (who was very proud of the Incan empire) was teaching us from an esoteric view, it was such a contrast. It was a great honour to be guided by him. After all, we were on a transformational journey and it gave me such pleasure to see the group growing and blossoming every day as they sat and soaked up every word that was taught. On our return to Cusco we would have a short siesta and then venture out for the evening, most times finding ourselves either in the main plaza or close by. There were so many delicious restaurants to choose from with fantastic food and, of course, the famous Peruvian musicians played to us while we ate, often getting us up to participate in dancing or playing one of their instruments. Tired to the bone with the long days, we could not have been happier.

This particular night I crashed onto my bed, wrapped myself up warmly, as the temperature dropped dramatically at night, and I drifted off to sleep. It was a restless night and, once again, I found myself in a very deep dream state where I was being introduced to three men and told they were my teachers. One of them was Willaru and and I did not know the other two. I saw their faces vividly and then the next thing I knew it was morning. Waking with a very sore neck and feeling as if I had not had any sleep, I wrote my notes in my diary. There was definitely something magical about the energy of Cusco, of Peru. These dreams that I was having were so clear and powerful. Was this all part of my transformational journey? Over the next few years I met the other two men in the dream and they were indeed incredibly profound teachers for me. I was flabbergasted that my dream had been so accurate and I often long to be back in the high vibration of Peru so that my soul can travel easily to the astral plane to have more of these life-changing experiences.

The group was feeling sad at having to say goodbye to Cusco but at the same time they were excited to finally be venturing into the Sacred Valley where a whole new adventure was awaiting them. Up at the crack of dawn, bags packed and loaded into the bus, we began the climb from Cusco town to the top of the mountain ridge where we would see the breath-taking view of the Sacred Valley in all of its glory, for the first time. Absolutely nothing can prepare you for this. It is truly spectacular in every sense of the word. With the Andes mountain range, snow capped and cradling the valley on either side, you just cannot keep your jaw from dropping as you soak it all in and at the same time sense the energy levels shifting up a gear or two. Winding slowly down from the ridge and into the valley itself there was lots of chatter and anticipation as we headed towards Pisac, the first village you encounter.

What you don't know won't hurt you.......

Willaru was busy telling us about the famous Pisac markets and there were shouts of excitement as we could see them in the distance. There was going to be some serious shopping done here that was for sure! There were row upon row of goods for us to barter for and then try

to fit into our suitcases. How long did we have? Only two hours! We would need more like two days! The first port of call before the shopathon was a fabulous café called Ulrike's run by a German woman who had been living there for many years. The food was simply divine and of course leaning more towards a European palate which suited us foreigners. Tummies full, laden down with shopping bags, especially after discovering the shaman's shop down one of the side streets, it was time to step out of the material world and back into the esoteric as we ventured up to the Pisac ruins to take a walk through the ancient mystery school that once was.

Walking single file, we began the climb along the steep and narrow path to the main part of the ruins that were precariously located on the side of the mountain. The sun was starting to slip away and the air was brisk. Zipping my jacket up and breathing hot air into my hands I heard the lone sound of a Peruvian whistle and sure enough, up ahead was a young boy, no more than ten, playing for us in the hope of getting a few coins. It was such a tough life they had. These kids lived deep in the Andean mountains and would walk at least one to two hours each way every day to school. It was a life that westerners found hard to comprehend. Watching our step with no handrails to hold onto and looking for a secure spot to stand and hand over a few coins, there it was, the most beautiful smile and eyes that shone with gratitude. Your heart just melted every time.

Nervous and anxious to get to the end of this winding path and more solid ground, we kept climbing one step at a time and then we hit a cave, which looked very uninviting. Thanks Willaru, I thought, the group will not be too happy about this. I had learnt one of the ways in which Willaru taught our clients how to face fear head on was to not pre-warn them about something that was going to be challenging. He said that if they knew, they would already have stepped into fear and admitted defeat without even trying. So here we were, having to crawl into a cave with no lighting and no end in sight. Head down, holding onto the person in front we all took one step at a time trusting and hoping that nothing untoward would jump out at us. Finally we saw daylight ahead.

Wow, the view from this ancient mystery school, what was left of it, was spectacular. You could imagine that the students and masters would have felt even closer to other realms and the source itself, being this high up with the Apus and mountain gods surrounding them. Standing and listening to Willaru teach us on gnostic theories, the 48 cosmic laws, the history of the school, the rooms, and what they were used for, the way in which they worked with the sundial and so much more, it was as if it was a scene from the past coming back to life. Willaru, was the master, and the rest of the group, the students. Having had time to meditate, we all gathered in one of the remaining rooms of the ruins and Willaru showed us how you could hear the musical note of the site, which determines the vibration of a space, by "toning" into the carved junctions in the stone walls. Amazing! The sound was incredible. So pure and so loud. We were always learning. At any time of the day, Willaru would come out with words of wisdom for us to digest and store away. It was as if he knew what was going on in each and everyone's lives as the subjects seemed to be so relevant. Every time I visited Peru he would find a moment when we were alone to share what seemed like

a message specifically for me. Like the time he talked to me about black and white magic and how a person can wear two faces. I had just had a very harrowing experience back in New Zealand that had left me a little weary. How did he know? Of course, he is an incredibly gifted man. Like the time I was standing in my lounge back in New Zealand and he came into my mind and told me there was going to be an earthquake. I thought nothing of it until the next day when the big one in Christchurch hit! He often tells me that we can and must talk in the astral plane. How lucky am I to have met this wonderful man?

Picking up the pace, as it had become very cold all of a sudden, we scrambled over the steps to the waiting bus, welcoming the warmth inside. One of the local ladies and her little baby jumped in and rode down the mountain with us. She couldn't wipe the smile off her face, getting a ride was like winning lotto!

Driving along the main road through the Sacred Valley was mesmerising as every few yards our eyes caught something new. There might be a long driveway leading down to what looked like a remote retreat or a bunch of local men sitting around drinking Chicha beer (the local brew made from corn), crops being tended to, women sitting in groups weaving and let's not forget the beautiful children. Muddy faced, ragamuffin clothes, happy as could be, and full of mischief. Combine all of this with the lush vegetation, commanding presence of the Andes and the warmth of the people. This certainly was a sacred valley.

Mystery Schools, so many questions and so little time…

Tonight we were staying in a little village called Rumichaka at Hosteria Rumichaka. What a find. Tucked away from the main road down a bumpy drive, was this gorgeous privately owned bed and breakfast accommodation with the most beautiful white huskies to greet us. The hosts were delightful and absolutely nothing was too much trouble. Hose and Irene, having lived in the USA for some time, knew how to impress. With Pisco sours, the famous national drink, waiting for us on arrival, in front of a roaring fire, what more could you ask for? Well, how about a four-course gourmet meal served by local Peruvian staff dressed in white jackets, bow ties and gloves?! Oh my goodness, we all thought we had died and gone to heaven!

After a delicious breakfast out on the deck, waiting for Willaru and the driver to turn up, we had a few moments to write in our journals. Everyone seemed very happy as today we were heading, via Urubumba and the local food market, (which was always so much fun), to Ollantaytambo a very impressive archeological site at the far end of the Sacred Valley. Entering the heart of the town via the one and only road made of cobblestones and only suitable for one-way traffic, was an adventure in itself. Crawling at 30 kms per hour we eventually arrived in the main square. Wow! This site cradled amongst the Andes Mountains at the end of the valley was massive, incredible, jaw dropping! Starting at ground level, Willaru guided us up the terraces bit by bit as he shared esoteric lessons from what was once a mystery school along with a smattering of the more conventional history. It felt like we were being

initiated into different dimensions the higher we went. It was a little bit of a challenge, especially for those who got short of breath easily. We were grateful that he was not like every other guide, rushing us straight up to the top. There was so much to observe and so many lessons to learn along the way.

On reaching the top, it became apparent that the Incans were disturbed before they could finish building the temple as there were two very large rose quartz stones standing solidly in place, leaving no doubt about this. Maybe they had been there well before Incan times, but if so, what was their purpose? There was no understanding or explanation as to where they really came from. The Spanish army could certainly not fathom out how to move them. Had they been placed there by the Lemurian race, highly spiritual beings at seven feet tall and known to be extremely advanced in the height of their civilisation, in what was once the Land of Mu. You really needed to spend weeks at the site, known as the Temple of the Heart in the esoteric world, as there were so many lessons to be taught at this ancient mystery school. Oh, how I wish I could live here for six months and have Willaru teach me each day on the intricacies of the way in which these temples were built and why the significance - of the number of doors, the positioning of stones and the series of steps and much more. We had only touched the surface.

Looking out across the valley to the other side of the mountain, Willaru explained that the set of ruins we could see, with an impressive façade still intact, was where those who were practicing at the mystery school went for their spiritual retreats. If we looked to the left of the remains there was an amazing sight to be seen. Carved naturally into the rock was the face of an Incan King. It was huge and there is no way it could have been manmade. It is a natural phenomenon that cannot be explained to this day. Standing there daydreaming about the times that were, Willaru brought me back as he beckoned us to follow him along the ridge and narrow mountain path as we wound our way around the mountainside reaching the Temple of the Condor, located opposite the carving of the Incan King. These temples had been specifically positioned and as we clambered up onto the sacred ledge, lying directly below the face of the condor in the rock, we could feel the spirit of the Incan King as well. In this very special place, deep in meditation, we were able to connect to the 5th dimension with the help of the condor. Closing my eyes and feeling myself slip down into that wonderful place where I found myself travelling between the realms and being shown many symbols I was rudely interrupted by a guard yelling at us to get down. We were told it was actually forbidden to spend time on the sacred ledge. Thank goodness we had disobeyed and managed to get some precious moments there as we had experienced the powerful connection.

That oh so familiar feeling...have I been here before?

Many questions were being fired at Willaru as we departed from the site to wander around the markets before we sat down for a light lunch and our next visit to a local native quero shaman. Sipping my pisco sour and waiting for my lunch to arrive, I noticed a gorgeous little Peruvian boy of about seven or eight years of age approaching me. He came up with a big smile on his face and wanted to play. Well, that was it, from that moment on he would not leave my side. It was as if he was my

own. It did not matter that we could not speak the same language as we shared laughter and lots of cuddles and played games. This country never ceased to surprise me with these precious moments and the true warmth of the people. It was time to leave, so one last cuddle for the beautiful little boy as we were moving on to visit Vidal, a local shaman at his own healing centre.

What a treat it was to be shown around the centre and have a special ceremony prepared for us. As we filed into the room we were given coca leaves and one by one led to the fire to release them while making a wish and setting an intention. Sitting in a circle with Vidal in the heart of it, the sacred water was passed around for each to drink as he completed the ceremony to welcome us home. I felt so incredibly happy I could have burst. Being in the right place at the right time reconnecting to a past life was surely what must be happening here. Then Vidal came up to me and said he could feel my happiness and in Spanish he exclaimed, “GRANDE GRANDE!” He said my ancestors were very pleased to have me here. How would I sleep tonight after this fabulous day and the prospect of finally reaching Machu Picchu tomorrow?

Seated on board our train packed with tourists, the atmosphere was one of anticipation. Departing from Ollantaytambo we sat back to enjoy the one and a half hour train ride through the most beautiful canyon where the Urubumba river ran precariously close to the tracks on more than one occasion. Winding around bend after bend with eyes glued to the window, time just flew by and before we knew it we were approaching Agues Callientes the famous town below the ancient site of Machu Picchu. It was a buzz of activity from the moment we stepped off the train with market sellers and their goods, locals trying to entice you to stay with them and porters wanting to carry your bags. The town was an eclectic mix of half finished buildings spreading out from the railway tracks and up the side of the valley. With steep lanes to climb and so many shops and restaurants to explore, as well as the hot baths at the very top of the village, we were going to be busy! Checking in and leaving our bags it was back down in the foyer to head off together for our first visit to Machu Pichhu!

Words cannot express the feelings, finally we were here…

Winding our way up the side of the mountain in one of the many buses that ran every 20 minutes, a life-time ambition for many in the group was coming to fruition. Machu Picchu, the lost city of the Incas, finally we were going to arrive. Handing over our passports and receiving the Machu Picchu stamp was a great way to enter the site. Watching the rest of the group, I could see that they were in absolute awe of actually being there. It would take some time to sink in. It did not matter how many times I returned to Machu Picchu, I always felt the same way. I remembered an old Quecha Indian proverb: "One day at a sacred site is worth a 1000 days of meditation." How true this was; magic in every sense of the word and, for many, a healing journey that was life changing.

There were many large groups of tourists following their guides. Looking at our small group I was forever grateful. We could all huddle around and listen closely. It was easy for us to stop at any time and

rest together, discuss a topic or meditate. This was the only way to see Machu Picchu and give it the respect that it deserved, with a small group, a spiritual leader and time. Many were just there for an afternoon and then they were back on the train to Cusco. We could take our time as we had all of tomorrow as well. Wandering the city, Willaru had us entranced as he shared so much of the ancient wisdom, pointing out aspects that no other group were being privy too. We discovered he had spent three months in the city, meditating every day. He knew it like the back of his hand. Walking slowly, we made our way past the funerary area and then took the long trail up to the Sun Gate, which is where the Inca trail trekkers climb over the rise to receive their first glimpse of the ancient city. It was a beautiful walk, meandering up the mountainside while sharing stories and teachings at the same time. Arriving at the Sun Gate the atmosphere was one of joy with so many trekkers resting, having a snack after their long climb to this point. The porters were rearranging the massive loads they carried and were grateful for any snack offered to them. I had so much respect for these young men. They were unbelievably strong, putting their own safety at risk and getting paid a pittance. Looking across at Waynu Picchu, which means “Young Mountain” and commenting on the fact that we would have the option to climb it tomorrow started one question after another for poor Willaru. Just as he said, if you gave people time to think about a challenge it inevitably created more fear than was necessary and the possibility of them not accepting the challenge at all.

Changing the subject I managed to get the group on our way again and we made our way back down into the ancient city. Up and down steps, we were learning about the many different parts of the city from a practical and spiritual point of view. How they lived, where the most important temples were located, such as the Temple of the Condor, and then further down at the edge of the city, we got the chance to ride the condor. There was a rock jutting out over a fairly steep drop and those who were brave enough lay across it on their stomachs, holding their arms out like wings so that you felt like you were flying. Balancing and looking straight across to Putukusi, another very large sacred mountain, you were to look for the door and a tunnel, the portal that would connect you to a higher dimension where the gods lived.

Wandering further around the site I noticed that all of a sudden there were fewer people – making it the best time of the day. Taking a path that was a little off the beaten track, Willaru led us to see an incredibly powerful stone located near the entrance of Waynu Picchu. There it was, a massive stone that had the faces of the two great indigenous tribes, the eagle of the north and the condor of the south. This was where the Incan prophecy was symbolically represented: "When the condor of the south comes together with the eagle of the north, the spirit of mother earth – Pacha Mama – will awake and then she will awaken millions of her children. This will be the resurrection of the dead." It was a power spot and the perfect place to absorb its energies as we sat quietly meditating. With only a short time left we spent the rest of it at one of the most significant parts of the hidden city. The sundial and its temple located in the heart of the city, in the most prestigious position to receive the first of the sun's rays. Many ceremonies, initiations, sacrifices and celebrations were held here in times gone past. Oh my goodness, I was seeing energy like I had never seen it before. Standing here I could see white balls of energy actually moving in a circular direction around our

group and across the mountains. The power of a sacred site! Whistles blowing and guards shouting at us we had five minutes before the gates would shut and the last bus would depart. Tired bones and scratchy eyes mattered not as we sat down on the bus for the winding trek back down to Agues Calientes. This is what we came for.

Out of the bus and climbing one of the lanes to our hotel, Willaru was suddenly approached by a beautiful gentleman waving his arms full of excitement. They embraced and began to talk feverishly in their native tongue. We stood patiently waiting until Willaru turned around and explained that the gods had brought them together at this precise moment. This wise elder standing in front of us was none other than grand Mayan elder Don Alejandro. He was here with an American film crew making a movie known as "The Great Shift" and they were travelling from North America down the coast of South America ending in Bolivia. Don Alejandro had woken up that morning and asked Spirit to connect him with an Incan elder. The fascinating thing was that Willaru and Don Alejandro had met about 10 years before at an indigenous conference in the USA but had lost contact. How amazing was that? Here they were, connecting again. It was arranged that after dinner that evening the two of them would sit in conversation to discuss and share the prophecies of both the Mayan and Incan races. How privileged we were, as we were invited to listen in. Even though they spoke in Spanish it did not matter as we knew that it was indeed a very special moment in time that was captured on film for the world to see.

We were up extremely early so that we could take the first bus up to Machu Picchu and see the sun rise. Winding up the side of the mountain it was different this time round as the mist was low and you could not see a thing. This was one of my absolute favourite ways to discover Machu Picchu, watching the mist lift as the hidden city was revealed in all of its glory. True to form, this magical ancient site did not let us down and before long, the sun was warming us up as we made our way across the hidden city to the entrance of Waynu Picchu. As we signed our names in the official book at the little booth where they manned the number of tourists climbing on a daily basis, I wondered if we were ready for this. Gulp, I hoped so. Many of the group had been anxious about taking the climb as it was a fair hike, steep and with no handrails to hold onto. Willaru was reassuring them and saying we did not need to rush like so many others. We would take it slowly, stopping at every corner to share a story or two. Off we set with Willaru chewing on one of the girl's bags of coca leaves to give him the extra bit of strength he needed, much to her disappointment, as she had wanted them herself! It was tough, the steps were deep and seemed to go on forever but with one foot in front of the other, before we knew it we had made it almost to the top. It was such a joy for me to see the sense of achievement, the conquering of fear on each and everyone's face. Only the last little bit to go. Weaving ourselves through what seemed like the eye of a needle we were at the top. With lots of large rocks, some with a sheer drop and everyone finding a spot to rest and refuel, you certainly felt like you were on top of the world! Cameras were clicking, we had made it. Yahoo!!! Breathing in the fresh air and attempting to walk down one of the sheer drops like a local I surprised myself. Others were scurrying down on their backsides while I was able to stand up and walk down. Maybe I had also been here before, as it came so naturally to me!!

Now it was decision time. Were we going to head back down to the main city or were we going to attempt to take the climb down to the Temple of the Moon? Most people either did not know about this temple or did not have time. Located 500m down the far side of Waynu Picchu mountain, once again it was not for the faint hearted but for those who were up for an adventure. With a unanimous yes, off we went. It was a nice change to be climbing down even though there were a few hairy moments where we really had to watch our footing. On reaching the temple of the moon we could see only two other tourists and were so glad to have made the trek down. With a series of caves that were carved directly into the rock face, featuring some of the finest stone work in Machu Picchu, we could only imagine what it must have been like in Incan times. I began to envisage what it must have been like with the full moon lighting up the night sky and ceremony and ritual taking place. It would have been so very powerful. Taking time to sit on what looked like a carved throne, meditating and feeling the energy, time just whizzed by and the next thing we found ourselves climbing another 300m up to Machu Picchu and the lost city. I heard mutterings under breaths wishing that they had not climbed down in the first place. There would be some very sore limbs tonight but in hindsight, they would be fully satisfied that they had achieved so much.

Medicine Women and their gifts...

It was with sadness that we had to say goodbye to Machu Picchu but there was always a plus side, there was another adventure around the corner. Today we were to take the train back to Ollantaytambo and then be collected by our driver and driven back to Cusco through the Sacred Valley one more time stopping at Pisac for some last minute shopping at the markets, a delicious lunch at Ulrike's Café and for me, the chance to spend some time with Wilma, a medicine woman who I had been told about. I was very excited as Wilma, a very talented young lady, not only worked with plant medicine but also read the coca leaves. We had arranged to meet while the others were shopping and I was to have a reading.

There she was, a beautiful young Peruvian woman with her smile beaming from one side of her face to the other. "Welcome Sharon," she said as she ushered me into a chair. "Shareen, my sister." I loved her accent and the way in which she pronounced my name. Warming to her immediately, we began to talk about her role as a shaman, a medicine woman and what she did. Having been brought up by the elders and spending far more time with people twice her age she was not interested in boyfriends, dancing and discos. Instead, she was continually learning the traditional ways. She was one incredibly wise woman for her age. She loved to teach the Munay-ki, a series of nine empowerment rites based on the initiatory practices of the Q'ero shamans of Peru. "Munay" in Quechua means "love and will" and ki is the Japanese word for energy. Combining them together it means the energy of love. I wish I'd had more time to spend with her to immerse myself in the Munay-ki teachings. Never mind, I promised myself when I came back on my next trip, I would make sure that we would definitely do something together. In the meantime, she began to unravel her blanket of coca leaves asking me to pick three bundles up, blow into them three times and then cast them across the blanket. She then began reading the leaves. Wow, she was good, really good. How did she know these things? "Sharon, you are a very sensitive woman, you always feel what is happening, what is

going on inside the people you meet and those around you. You have very healing hands, oh my goodness, uno, dos, tres, cuatro, cinco. Yes cinco/five generations as a healer. It is in your blood, your DNA. You are part of us darling, part of this path. You are a medicine woman. You like to help many people and sometimes they do not respond." I laughed, she was right. I had had my fair share of helping people and being let down or chastised, to find out later on that they had indeed appreciated it, but were not ready to accept or admit it at the time. As a healer, and someone who always spoke the truth, I found one of my greatest lessons was that some of the people who crossed my path were not yet ready to hear what I had to share, or maybe, I needed to learn to keep it to myself until the time was right.

"My sister Shareen, what was the special dream you had while you have been here?" I stopped in my tracks and looked at her. Really, how did she know this? I had not mentioned it to anyone, a little embarrassed to do so, thinking that the others would say I was going mad or maybe showing off. A few nights back I had woken from a very deep dream where an ascended master had appeared. Truly, Lord Lanto, the master whose prime interest is in offering assistance to those who felt drawn to greater learning and the gaining of wisdom. His beautiful old face smiled at me and was showing me how to bring my thoughts to my third eye, then like oil being poured from a very small jug, let them filter down to the heart. I was told he was an ascended master from the second solar ray. For some time now, when I had these dreams I would grab my iPhone and in a half asleep state, write what I saw in the notes section to look at when I finally awoke. I knew this time that I would have to research this one.

Wilma mentioning this, confirmed to me that it was indeed not a fallacy, as how would she have known about my dream? All too soon, my time with her came to an end after her amazing insights and confirmations. Wow, wait until I told the others. Oh, maybe I shouldn't as they would all want to see her and we didn't have enough time.

Secret portals and magic messages…

On the last leg of our journey, (with just three nights left in the high altitude town of Puno), we were travelling from Cusco to Puno which entailed an all day trip with a stop at the Raqchi, the world's largest Inca temple ruins. They were incredible in stature with Inca stonework covering the first 13 feet in height and adobe adorning the rest. Built by the Incas in the 15th century it had once had a very large community with a thriving mystery school. Walking around the ruins I found it fascinating that each of the original homes were circular. It confirmed so much of the Feng Shui principals I had been taught via Denise Linn's Interior Alignment school of Feng Shui. It was very clear to me why I resonated with this school as it based many of its teachings upon the ancient wisdom and practices of more than one indigenous culture. My tours and these teachings went hand in hand, complementing each other.

Finally arriving in Puno you couldn't help but notice that you had definitely climbed in altitude by the start of a dull headache and shortness of breath. Man it was cold outside! I had been nodding in and out of sleep on the bus and woke to be shown where we would be heading the next day. I knew it was a special site, a temple in the shape of the Incan cross and I was also shown the animal symbols of a dog and an owl. Shortly after that I had seen a bunch of dogs running on the road and as we pulled up at the hotel I wasn't too surprised to see that the hotel's symbol was an owl. I was forever grateful that my third eye was opening up more and more due to the high vibration, allowing me to strengthen my gift of seeing. After a lovely traditional meal at a restaurant close by, accompanied by a local mariachi band, it was an early night all round. Jumping into bed I found there were two hot water bottles tucked inside. Now that was great service!

It was our second to last day, one that I had a feeling we would not forget in a hurry. On board our coach with Willaru and local guide Rebecca, we were heading out into the countryside to what seemed like the middle of nowhere. I couldn't help but notice how clean and peaceful the countryside looked. The people may not have much by way of material possessions but they were happy. Pulling up in a remote spot we got out and began another climb – which, by this time, some of the group were not crazy about. They were getting a little tired as we were nearing the end of the trip. Rebecca was telling us how the temple we were about to spend time at, was a representation of the seven chakras. Along the path there were huge obelisk stone carvings positioned in what seemed like strategic places. One more bend and we had made it to the top and it was amazing. What blew me away was the fact that this was the place I had seen yesterday, when I woke up on the bus as I drifted in and out of sleep. It had once been in the shape of the Incan cross and in the centre was a large circle with entrances from about six different points. There was a sun gate to the left of the circle, which is where the sun's rays hit. The rays were then transported by ley lines through to the likes of Machu Picchu and the other energy points around planet earth.

Back on the bus and still driving alongside Lake Titicaca we were heading towards the Temple of Amara Muru. Walking towards the temple itself, constructed by mother nature, it was striking indeed. Immediately you could tell it was a very special place. The whole side of a mountain with the body of two serpents, the head of a serpent and the condor on top was so impressive. Half way along the side of the mountain there was what looked like an Incan door that had been carved into the mountain and on either side of the door were two rectangular panels carved into the rock from the ground right up to the top of the mountain. It was notable as the mountain was so high and the door was human height. Such a contrast. We were told the door was an inter-dimensional portal, a star gate. Willaru stood and talked to us, reiterating much of what he had taught us over the past few weeks, reminding us about the ego, the temple of the heart and how we needed to practice every day in bringing our ego down to the internal mother/fire of our heart where we could burn it. Guiding us one by one to stand inside the portal door facing the mountain ensuring our forehead touched the rock and as much of the rest of our body as we could, we were given individual time to close our eyes and take in the experience.

I was transported immediately to another space and time. I saw a very large (what I thought at first was an) animal as it was very tall on two legs but realised was a human. The next thing I saw was this huge eye just staring straight back at me. I kept seeing snakes and felt like I was being transported down a tunnel. The connection was very strong and

I kept being drawn into this other world. Stepping away from the door I let the next person have their turn. Sitting quietly on a rock, while waiting for everyone to finish I was trying to fathom what had just happened. Then Willaru asked me to read an excerpt from a book that one of the ladies had bought with her. He had been so excited when he saw it, as it was now out of print, 'Brother Phillips, Secret of the Andes.' I started reading and then I froze. No way! It was talking about the first race to come to earth, the Cyclopean race. They were extremely tall and had one eye!! This was exactly what I had just seen a few moments ago standing in the portal. Until this moment I had never heard of the Cyclopean race. I was ecstatic, over the moon, what a way to end my trip to Peru by having this experience.

It was with a lightness in my heart, a spring in my step and a much deeper understanding of a world around us that I was heading home to New Zealand. My expanded awareness of this vast, miraculous, mysterious world we live in, I knew, meant life would probably never be the same again.

CHAPTER SEVEN:

Destiny

CHAPTER SEVEN:

Destiny

Curled up in my favourite armchair, a piping hot cup of coffee and journal in hand I was settling in for a good read as I took a trip down memory lane. Reflecting back, I thought about how so much had happened since that first life-changing trip to Egypt all those years ago. Turning the pages I was captivated immediately as once again I began to relive the adventures.

Trust in your intuition and dreams…..

Having spent the first night in Shanghai, we arrived in Chengdu and were very grateful to be spending the next few nights in a much smaller city as we waited for the Rinpoche to arrive so that we could begin our adventure high into the Tibetan mountains. Shanghai had been fascinating with a mixture of the old and the new. Skyscrapers, modern technology, department store after department store with a heavy western influence and, if you were lucky, you might get to spot the occasional park and traditional teahouse. The number of people walking the streets at any one time was quite incredible. The crowds were at least 10 deep, row after row, and god forbid, if you wanted to stop and tie your shoelaces! Yes, Jenny and I were very happy to wander this sleepy town of Chengdu, stocking up on our snacks as we negotiated for fruit and nuts with the local vendors, sampling the delicious food and resting a little before our whirlwind week in Tibet started.

Larger than life, a very special man with such warmth, compassion and intelligence, Rinpoche Amnyi Trulchung was striding towards us in the hotel foyer, to grab our bags and introduce us to his brother Sochi who was to be our driver for the next week. Rinpoche means "precious one," and that he was. He was such an extremely well educated and personable man who had committed his life to representing his Buddhist lineage and working tirelessly for his people. One minute he would have us in fits of laughter and the next we knew we were in the presence of a great teacher and holding onto every word of wisdom that he shared.

Heading out into the car park, Sochi behind the wheel, a younger version of the Rinpoche, Jenny and I both shot a quick glance at each other. True to form, and just as we had expected, the car was pretty old but it looked comfortable enough and it was obviously Sochi's pride and joy. Jumping in the back, suitcases loaded into the trunk we began the very long journey to the town of Sershul in the Sichuan province of Tibet. It was going to take a couple of 8-10 hour days of driving to get there. We hoped it wouldn't be too boring.

No chance of that! With bouts of singing and laughter, serious discussions about the world, life and the human psyche accompanied by long moments sitting with our own thoughts, staring out of the window at the most spectacular scenery, it was breathtaking! I loved this place so much. The sky was the bluest I had ever seen, the air was so fresh, the colours and shapes of the mountains stunning as they went for mile upon mile. Every now and then, dotted on the horizon you might see a small bunch of trees, the only piece of greenery to be seen in hours, oh how we appreciated it. Winding up and over steep passes and then down onto the valley floor the time just flew by. Stopping for lunch in one of the many villages we drove through, it was fascinating. It was market day and there was lots of activity in town with everyone selling their wares and stocking up. The fresh produce was amazing. There were rows and rows of meat, vegetables, fruits, grains and spices. Looking down the street I noticed the funniest of things. Outside the restaurants or shops there were cars, motorbikes and horses parked up alongside each other!! Yes horses! There were still plenty of Tibetans who chose a horse as their form of transport, especially the nomads who lived in the mountains.

Poor old Jenny, she wasn't feeling too well and I hoped she wasn't getting altitude sickness. She had been so excited to be able to join me on this week of exploration. The Rinpoche and I were hoping to put a tour to Tibet together in the future and I had taken this opportunity to see what his village and monastery were like and how he would fare as a tour guide. We were close to arriving in Sershul, his home town, about 4,500m above sea level and it was pretty obvious poor Jen would be heading straight to bed.

On our arrival, the children came running and there were many handshakes and much slapping on the back, hugs and talking. It was obvious that the Rinpoche was dearly loved and highly respected by his people. They were very excited to have him back even if it was only for a few days. Drawn swiftly away by what looked like senior members of the community, I was not to see him much over the next few days as he attended meetings from dusk till dawn. Left to my own devices I soon made friends with some of the ladies, even if it was with sign language and lots of smiles. I wandered the town, poked around in the shops and came across some hair-raising sights like the local dentist in his space, which was the size of a cupboard, with no doors, and open to anyone on the street to get a bird's eye view. As you can imagine, the

equipment was archaic and some poor bugger was in the chair having a tooth extracted for all and sundry to see! The rest of the time was spent with Jenny and trying to lessen the pain she was going through. Thank goodness I had not come down with altitude sickness. I had been unlucky enough to have had it in Peru a few times and it was horrible.

The few days went really quickly with visits to the Ju Mohor Monastery to see the results of the Vista Project firsthand, a project that the Rinpoche had been tirelessly working on. With great dedication and determination, the project was in place and doing well in revitalising the economic and cultural lives of the Tibetan people.

Before we knew it, we were back in Soshi's car and heading towards Chengdu once again. At least Jenny was feeling a little better but still not eating much. Jenny was one of the most generous and giving people I had ever had the pleasure of meeting and she had been so looking forward to playing with the children and helping the elderly. Never mind I told her, next time!! There would certainly be a next time.

Pulling over in the middle of nowhere for something to eat I noticed that there were horses tied up outside a building and they were cooking over a fire. As soon as we entered the building with the Rinpoche, people came running from nowhere. Next thing we were ushered into a private room with lots of fuss and pomp while we waited for the food to be served. Something inside was niggling at me, I didn't really want to eat or maybe I shouldn't eat. However, as Jenny was recovering from her altitude sickness and the people were obviously going out of their way because of the Rinpoche, I felt obligated to eat. Oh my god, I wish I had listened to my intuition! It would have saved much heartache and pain.

I would say it was 5 hours or so and then it hit. Diarrhoea, an incredibly strong bout of it that just did not stop for days!! It was my turn to be laid up in bed 24/7 only getting up to say hello to the toilet when I had to! Oh, the trials and tribulations of travelling in a foreign land. Come hell or high water I was getting on that plane back to NZ. I needed my own bed, some medicine that worked fast and real food. The power of the mind is a wonderful thing. I got on that plane and made it back home.

Taking a few weeks to adjust back into a normal rhythm I still had a niggling feeling that something was not quite right. I was so very lethargic and feeling bloated most of the time. I wondered what was wrong. Just putting it down to one too many red wines I carried on with life until the morning I awoke from one of my "powerful" dreams. In the dream, I was at the doctors in Sydney being told I had Hepatitis E and it was from the water in Tibet. How strange?! The familiar groggy feeling was there as I pulled myself out of the deep dream state. Stumbling out of bed I dragged myself to the computer and immediately googled Hepatitis E. Was there such a thing? Sure enough there was and its cause was from contaminated water. I knew there and then that whatever I had eaten at that lunch stop on the way back to Chengdu was contaminated and I was suffering from this. How on earth do you tell a doctor that this is what is wrong with me because I was told in my dreams?

Visiting not one but a few doctors I soon found out that they could do the blood test for Hepatitis E but the samples had to go to Sydney! Wow, that was the second confirmation that the dream was indeed very real. What was I to do? They had done a selection of tests but not the Hepatits E one and nothing had been discovered. In the end, I visited a fabulous herbalist who immediately told me I did have a strain of Hepatitis and

the doctors often missed it with their blood tests. Thank goodness, I started feeling a lot like my old self but I had noticed (and once again my intuition was telling me), whatever the bug was, it had attacked my reproductive system as my cycle just seemed to stop abruptly. As a healer, I knew deep down inside that there must have been a reason why this had happened. It would intrigue me for many years as I tried to fathom out what might have been happening on an emotional level at that time that would put me in that position.

To top my suspicions off, the Rinpoche on his return to New Zealand not long after myself, had gone into silent retreat for 30 days. The day it finished he rang me to see how I was and started the conversation with, "There is one place we will not return to Sharon, is that right?" I did not need to tell him, he must have picked up on what was happening while in silent retreat. Yet another confirmation that my dream had revealed what had happened.

The power of family.....

I had not noticed the light starting to fade out as day turned to night – so absorbed was I in my journal and my memories. I was in heaven, not wanting the memories to end. Emotions were flowing freely, one minute laughing and the next tears running down my face. The people I had met along the way, lovers, friends for life, even enemies, some of them my greatest teachers. Would I change anything? Never, each and every one of the experiences had enriched my life and helped me grow into a stronger and wiser woman. I laughed to myself as I thought some might disagree with that analogy.

Turning the page, I was rapidly transported back to my time in the Arnhem Land where one thing seemed to happen after another. I will never forget the drive from Darwin through to Gove as we travelled across one of the largest Aboriginal reserves in Australia. Anthea, Heather and I were sitting in the back of the 4 wheel drive with our tour guides in the front. We were a small group with the three musketeers in the back and the (soon to be discovered) novices in the front. The three of us were so excited. Finally we were together and were heading across this vast stretch of land to our final destination, one of the coastal peninsulas of Gove, where we were to spend time with the Aboriginal healing women.

With the sun shining, red soil and dust as far as you could see, gum tree after gum tree, with their blue haze silhouetted on the horizon and a wild animal appearing every now and then – the never-never land had cast us under its spell. Driving and driving and driving, it just seemed to go on forever. Tonight we were to spend the evening at a campground in one of the small towns en route. Finally arriving around 7 pm, we pulled up outside the camping ground to find the whole thing locked up with no life at all. What were we going to do? Sitting in the back like quiet wee mice we waited to hear the guide's decision. No problems, we would carry on driving for a bit and set up our own camp in about an hour's time. The three of us looked at each other sideways. What??? It was getting dark and we were starving.

Driving through one of the many creek beds and up the other side, the main guide suddenly pulled the vehicle over and decided this was where we were to camp for the night. It was on the edge of a bank just above the creek. Head torches on, gear flying out of the vehicle we were hastily trying to erect our tents in what was now the darkness of night, in the middle of bloody nowhere. Famished, we finally got to sit around the campfire and eat. Nerves were on a high as we had exchanged whispered conversations between the three of us. Do these two know what they are doing? Totally exhausted after our first day of adventure it was almost time to leave the safety of the campfire and jump into our own tents for the night. Having held on for as long as I could I now really needed to have that final ablution stop. We had been told, if it was number two, that you needed to take the shovel with you, dig a hole and cover it up afterwards so as not to attract any of the wildlife! Charming! It was a bit of a challenge for us city girls.

So off I strode out into the back of beyond with just my head torch and a full bowel. Finding my spot and crouching down about to do my business I hear across the night sky – turn off your torch, turn off your torch!!! What the heck?

I can't turn it off what if there is a snake lurking out there or some other frightening beast? I would be a prime target! There was a large truck hurtling towards us from a distance on the one and only road and the tour guide was scared that if they saw life they might stop and cause us more trouble than good. Shit, I supposed I'd better turn my torch off. I was terrified. Needless to say, all thoughts of releasing my bowels were forgotten as I crouched in the dark waiting for the truck to pass.

Up with the first rays of sunlight and totally relieved that we had survived the night, we noted how close we had been to the creek where crocodiles lived!! Maybe these guides were not to be trusted. They had just put all of our lives at risk. We would have to investigate a little more. Packed up, fed and watered, it was back on the road for the remainder of the journey across the Arnhem Land in daylight hours, we hoped.

Unbelievably, the same but worse played out once again! Night had fallen, the beachside camping spot we were heading to was close but getting to it meant we had to drive down the steepest, potholed road I had ever been on. Thank god we had a 4 wheel drive. Holding on for dear life as we flew over bump after bump we finally made it to flat ground. Hopping out of the vehicle, Anthea and Heather exclaimed immediately, no way! We are not staying here for the night, it is far too dangerous. They insisted we get back in the vehicle and be driven to the closest town! You could have cut the air with a knife but I was ever so glad that they had spoken out.

In the distance we could see lights, finally signs of a town and comfort, we hoped. Pulling up at the one and only motel that we could find we were told it must have been our lucky night. Due to a power outage, rooms were filling up and we managed to get the last two. Someone was looking after us!! Dropping our bags it was down to the local pub where they had a generator and the restaurant was still operational for a much needed wine and meal. This spiritual adventure was turning out to be like an episode of Faulty Towers.

Maybe all would be well now that we had reached our destination. Today we were to meet the Aboriginal healing women with whom we would be living for the next three days. There they were, waiting for us in the car park, all four generations of them, ranging in age from 5 through to 60! Oh what stories they would have to share. Piling our gear onto their truck and ourselves into the back we began the slow

and laborious ride to their idyllic piece of paradise at the far end of the peninsula. It was pretty tough, getting stuck in the sand a few times. Nothing a bunch of aboriginal women couldn't fix; they were old hands at this. It was so beautiful to spend time with these ladies hearing their stories, feeling their pain and experiencing their joy all rolled into one. They were strong, tough and forthright even down to the little one, but they had to be. They had to survive. Settled in the most glorious bay with white sand, crystal clear water and big trees to shade themselves we understood why it was so important for them to retain their heritage and their land.

Over the next three days we sang, we danced, we learnt about the plants, we ate fresh fish from the bay and we listened to these wise women share intimate information about their lives. It was so apparent that everything they did was based around 'family.' Nothing was more important than family. I felt the tears lurking just below the surface a few times but I managed to squash them back down. Why was I feeling so emotional? Then it dawned upon me, spending the last three days in the energy of this 'big family' and seeing the way in which the old looked after the young and the young looked after the old had touched a nerve. Not having my own children and being in this loving environment made me a little sad inside.

Waking on what was to be our last morning I felt a familiar pain in my stomach. No, surely not. I hadn't felt this for quite some time. How amazing, it was the return of my menstrual cycle! What had triggered this? Immediately I knew. The bond of family, especially of woman in a healing space such as this, had somehow awakened and nurtured my reproductive system, bringing it into balance once again.

How grateful I was for that morning back in New Zealand when I was prodded with such force as I lay sleeping. I remember it distinctly, I had been wondering as I drifted in and out of sleep whether I should travel to the Arnhem Land or not. Then there it was, the prod with such force out of nowhere that it woke me up with a start, reassuring me that I must go.

A pilgrim trail also known as the walk of love……

Nearing the end of the journals with just one section to go I jumped up and poured myself a glass of red wine, settling back into my chair to savour the last of the stories.

How many times had I walked the Camino de Santiago trail? Too many for me to remember! Each time I loved it more than the last, always noticing something different, never tiring of the scenery, the culture, the food or the wine! Every day was a delight and the people I met along the trail were so precious. Walking in the footsteps of the tens of thousands of pilgrims who had walked the path since the middle ages I found myself imagining what it must have been like, way back then. It was legend that if you walked this ancient route as a pilgrim all your sins would be forgiven. I surely hoped so!

Winding back to the very first time on the trail it was a love affair right from the start. Call it luck or fate but it turned out that there were just the two of us, my girlfriend Kerin and I, on our departure! Actually the company had made a real boo boo and had forgotten to cancel our departure. Realising too late, as we had already paid our deposit, they had to honour our tour. How spoilt we were! Not one guide but two! It turned out that the woman who owned the company would be with us

for the first three days and then a second guide would join us for the last four.

Right from the start we fell in love with the trail. Loved, loved, loved it!

Each day we were up early for breakfast, sampling the treats and chatting to the other pilgrims before we took off, never knowing what sort of terrain we were to traverse. "Buen Camino," meaning have a "good way" or have a "good walk," rang out as we left for the day's adventures. Judy, our first guide and owner of the company we were travelling with, shared her story as we were walking the trail. We asked how she ended up here! Hailing from the USA and over on one of their long summer breaks she was booked to walk the trail with friends. Little did she know it was to be such a life-changing experience! Not only did she fall in love with Spain, its people, culture, and so much more, she met her future husband on the trail and love blossomed as they walked towards Santiago de Compostela. Here she was, eight years later, married and the owner of a Walking Tour Company, offering tours on the trail. It sounded like bliss to Kerin and I. Maybe it was fate, maybe these two souls were meant to meet on the trail.

Day thirty-nine of my forty day fast, phew! Just before I had left New Zealand, John of God, one of the most powerful mediums and healers alive today, had come to Wellington and I had attended his weekend event. The end result was that I received spiritual healing and it was suggested that I refrain from alcohol and a few other pleasures in life for forty days for it to really work! Always up for a challenge and wanting to respect the healing work and allow my physical and spiritual bodies to receive the highest energy and results I committed to the 40 days.

Talking to myself I said, ok, if I see a restaurant in the town we are staying in tonight that has paella on the menu, then I will have wine tonight and finish the fast. Lo and behold, a few moments down the street there was the sign I had secretly been wishing for.

Tonight we were swapping guides, Judy was leaving and Ricardo was replacing her. Kerin and I were looking forward to meeting him and sharing that delicious paella and wine! There he was, walking into the restaurant and up to the table greeting us all like long lost friends. What a charming man, such a character. We were going to have a lot of fun with him! He was such a great storyteller and not too bad on the eye either!! These Spanish men certainly knew how to put on the charm. There was something familiar about Ricardo but I could not put my finger on it. Never mind, I'm sure it would come to me over the next day or two.

Fast finished, the Spanish way of life and wine at lunchtime, I think I was happy! Ha, ha, we were having such a blast. We just loved meeting all the people along the trail and hearing their stories. Some sad, some humorous and some did not have a story, they were just there to walk the trail. That was why it was so special. Hearing stories of sadness where someone had passed over and the pilgrim was walking for them or someone who was extremely ill back home, they were walking for them, or maybe a pilgrim was celebrating and walking just for themselves.

Ricardo , Rico, Richard whatever we wished to call him was busy making sure that we stopped at all the best places to sample the food and taste the local delicacies. While we did this he entertained us with his vast array of knowledge on any topic we questioned him on. Under his spell

we were both listening and lapping up every word. He was explaining that in fact, the walk in pagan times was a kind of fertility route and that the word 'shell' – concha in south American Spanish, which has often retained the meanings of old Spanish words, refers to the female sexual organ. Taking it a step further he then shared the theory in pagan mythology about the sun-god making love to the sea-goddess in the twilight at the western most point of the earth. The memory of that act is the shell Venus-Aphrodite, the goddess of love. He certainly had me thinking. There were so many theories, so many beliefs and this is what was so special about the Camino. It was very much an internal journey while you indulged in all of the external delights.

How could life get any better than this? Great company, great food, great wine and a countryside to walk through that offered something new around every bend. One moment we were walking through ancient oak forests, then we were entering a hamlet where the locals were farming the fields and going about their business and the next we stumbled across a coffee stop full of lively pilgrims. Did this have to stop?? Next time it would be for longer; in hindsight, a week was far too short.

Striding out for the last part of the day, in the height of the heat, Kerin and I were deep in our own thoughts. Noting the bright splashes of wild flowers and the honesty stall up ahead, selling homegrown drinks, jams and fruit from the orchard, I stopped in the middle of my tracks. Yes, of course, that was how I knew him. I realised in that moment that Ricardo was one of the three teachers I had been shown in one of my powerful dreams a few years back in Peru. At the time of the dream I knew one of the teachers and that was Willaru, my Peruvian tour guide but the other two I had not met. Here I was, standing in the middle of the Camino trail in northern Spain with that niggling feeling of familiarity I had been questioning, confirmed. Wow, how amazing. There was definitely something special between us, I felt like I had known him for such a long time. Maybe it was a past life reconnection? Little was I to know that Ricardo and I were to become the best of friends, creating and selling our own walking tours along the Camino; he, as our legendary guide in Spain, and I as the tour co-ordinator, based on the other side of the world. Definitely one of my greatest teachers, he had the ability to drive me crazy. Crazy with affection as we shared laughter, a love of people and a constant need to have fun in this life and crazy with frustration as he challenged me on many things. He was forever the philosopher, forever one of my greatest teachers in life. I loved him to bits.

Placing the precious journals back in the cupboard I sat down to have that last cup of tea before heading to bed. Every day, yes, every day I still pinch myself and ask if this really is my life. It has been such an adventure. How was I to know at the tender age of 18 that my career in the travel industry was my destiny, my apprenticeship for what I had really come here to do? Travelling the world to the ancient sites and having all of these amazing experiences has led me down the path of the Shaman, of the healer reconnecting me with my many past lives. There have been too many co-incidences, too many times in my healing room when I have been shown lives gone past for clients. Having never met them before and finding out the connection between the information coming through and their current life situation was confirmation. I would never have believed in past lives if I had not had these opportunities to explore the greater mysteries in life firsthand.

For quite a few years I had wondered how I could combine my love of the business world, the human psyche and all of the information I had learnt when travelling around the world and working with people until I stumbled across the world of Feng Shui. I reflected on how lucky I had been to find the Interior Alignment School of Feng Shui. Drawn immediately to this school because of their deep understanding of the wisdom keepers around the world I knew I had found the last piece of the puzzle. It was a perfect fit.

Jumping into bed and snuggling even deeper under the covers, waiting for the dreamtime once again, I remembered back to my time with Wilma, the coca leaf reader in Peru, and her parting words.

"Shareen my sister, you must go, you must go to towns very far away, around the world to reawaken and collect the seeds. Collect the pure essence, the pure energies and take people there. You are a medicine woman. Always work with Munay, which is love and compassion. You must go."

As I fell deeper into the sleep time I heard myself making a promise to the universe, knowing that I had found my deeper purpose. I promised I would collect the seeds and share the wisdom collected from many of the mystical corners of the world through my love of being a tour guide, a Feng Shui Master Teacher, and an intuitive healer. I would teach wherever I could, at every opportunity I had.That was my destiny.

Authors Final Word

I have been to the ends of the earth, I have been to the ends of the waters, I have been to the ends of the sky, I have been to the ends of the mountains, I have found none that are not my friends. (Navajo Proverb)

About The Author

Travel expert, Interior Alignment Feng Shui master teacher, intuitive healer, and author, Sharon Breslin's life has been a full and exciting journey – both physically and spiritually.

Today she combines the experience of a lifetime of travelling with her work as owner and guide for Lifestyle Journeys Ltd, a Feng Shui practitioner and Interior Alignment School of Feng Shui master teacher.

The travel wanderlust started for Sharon, a native New Zealander, when her New Zealand mother and Irish father took her by ship, at the age of four, to live in England and Ireland for two years.

After returning to Wellington, the family shared a home with Sharon's uncle and his two very young children as he had tragically lost his wife. The family moved repeatedly as Sharon's father would build and sell properties but they eventually settled in Wellington.

Upon completing her education, through to qualifying to enter university, Sharon decided that the travel industry and the opportunity for excitement and adventure was definitely for her. She began her 25 year career in the industry, starting as a junior and working her way up to management level during which time she enjoyed many globe-trotting business-related excursions.

Her first position was with Variety Travel and then with her husband at the time she moved to London and worked in the travel industry, making the most of every opportunity to explore the northern hemisphere.

Returning to New Zealand, Sharon took on a senior travel consultant's position at AA Travel and then a short time later she joined the House of Travel Group in 1992 as a part-owner of one of the retail franchised outlets. She built the business from nothing to a 15-man operation over 13 years.

Right from the start it was a success, winning "Best New House of Travel" in its first year of operation. She also won the "Business Excellence Award" a few years later and in 2004 "Supreme Outlet Award," which was no mean feat when competing with the 90 outlets in the group at the time.

In her spare time, Sharon pursued her true passion, which was to learn about the metaphysical side of life. She discovered that she had been given a gift as an intuitive healer and was able to help many people.

She sold her travel franchise and co-founded a small tour company called Spiritual Journeys organising and leading trips to sacred sites and ancient lands around the world. When she and her business partner went their separate ways, Sharon rebranded the company as Lifestyle Journeys. Running it on a smaller boutique basis enabled her to spend the next 8 years doing more intuitive healing work from her home, as well as explore the world and continue the learning process by attending courses in various subjects—a psychic children's conference in Hawaii with James Twyman, a past life regression course in Virginia, USA with

Henry Bolduc, a past life regression course with Delores Cannon in New Zealand and a series of Feng Shui practitioner courses with the Interior Alignment School of Feng Shui, founded by Denise Linn and based in the USA.

Sharon then created another business which now sits alongside Lifestyle Journeys, called Feng Shui Spaces. A platform for showcasing her Feng Shui skills and along with all of the other tools she has acquired over the years, it focuses on assisting companies to look at their business from a new perspective, teaching them how to transform their business from "the inside out."

Sharon is the author of *Magical Travels - a travel guru's guide to the most mystical and amazing places on earth*.

Relocating herself and her businesses to Melbourne, Sharon has settled into a beautiful part of the city, Albert Park where she works from her studio promoting the tours, Feng Shui consultations/teaching, workshops and intuitive healing work.

Resources

HOW TO CONTACT SHARON BRESLIN

LIFESTYLE JOURNEYS: Based in Melbourne, VIC, Australia

Our mission at Lifestyle Journeys is to give you the travel experience of your life. As a boutique tour company and provider, we'll give you an experience that fulfills the potential of travel to amaze, move and transform. We would love to have you join us on one of our future tours. Take a look at our website to find the latest tour information:

www.lifestylejourneys.com
Sharon@lifestylejourneys.com
0061 3 9939 4272

Feng Shui Spaces: Melbourne, VIC, Australia

Feng Shui Spaces is a boutique consultancy created by the demand of individuals and companies seeking guidance and a deeper understanding of their environment and those who occupy the space within it. Sharon takes her key attribute – "holistic vision" – and offers it as a vital business tool for entrepreneurs looking for a powerful leap at any stage, both in business and their personal lives.

Professional Training Courses:

There has never been a more important time in our world to become a Feng Shui practitioner and Sacred Space professional. Take a look at our website to find the latest details on our certification programs and workshops.

www.fengshuispaces.com
Sharon@fengshuispaces.com
0061 3 9939 4272

TRAVEL:

Spencer Travel Group: Travel Specialists, Sydney, NSW, Australia

The Spencer Travel Group offers solutions for all travel needs providing first class service that has won them a multitude of awards over the past 10 years. They are continually finding ways to better enhance your travel experience and add value to their services.

www.spencertravel.com.au
contact@spencertravel.com.au
0061 2 9281 5477

ASTROLOGY:

If you want to learn more about yourself, why certain things have happened in your life and where you might be heading, then I highly recommend an astrological chart reading. Every time I am amazed at the accuracy of the chart and the guidance I receive.

Linda George: Evolutionary Astrologer based in Wellington New Zealand

www.cosmicride.wordpress.com

lindastrologer@gmail.com

Sylvia Flimm: Astrologer based on the Gold Coast, Queensland, Australia

Sylvia@ozemail.com.au

CLAIRVOYANT:

Patricia Treadaway: Clairvoyant based in Auckland, New Zealand

There are times in your life when you just need that special piece of guidance.

This wonderful lady has a gift whereby she can give you just that.

www.clairvoyantauckland.co.nz
patriciahealingyou@outlook.com

HYPNOTHERAPIST:

Holistique Hypnotherapy: based in Melbourne, VIC, Australia

Hypnotherapy is a form of psychotherapy that is used to create unconscious change in an individual. Olya uses hypnotherapy to assist individuals to improve their lives.

www.holistiquehypnotherapy.com
olya@holistiquehypnotherapy.com

FENG SHUI:

The Interior Alignment® School of Feng Shui: Worldwide

Interior Alignment® is a Feng Shui and space clearing system that embraces a holistic, intuitive approach bringing together the best of the mystical traditions of the east and native cultures around the globe and the practical modern methods of the west, uniquely combining the principles of Feng Shui, space clearing, sacred ceremony, healthy homes and the power of intention.

www.interioralignment.com

Rosemary Nelson: Feng Shui Landscape Designer based in Wellington, New Zealand

Combining her training via the Interior Alignment® School of Feng Shui with her wealth of knowledge in both landscape design and business, Rosemary is the perfect Feng Shui consultant to work with.

https://www.facebook.com/pages/Equate/380547705334171

HOLISTIC MAGAZINE:

Living Now Magazine: distributed throughout Australia

The Living Now magazine is a holistic, metaphysical directory and resource centre for personal development.
www.livingnow.com.au
advertising@livingnow.com.au

Edgar Cayce's Association for Research and Enlightenment: based in Virginia Beach, VA USA

www.edgarcayce.org

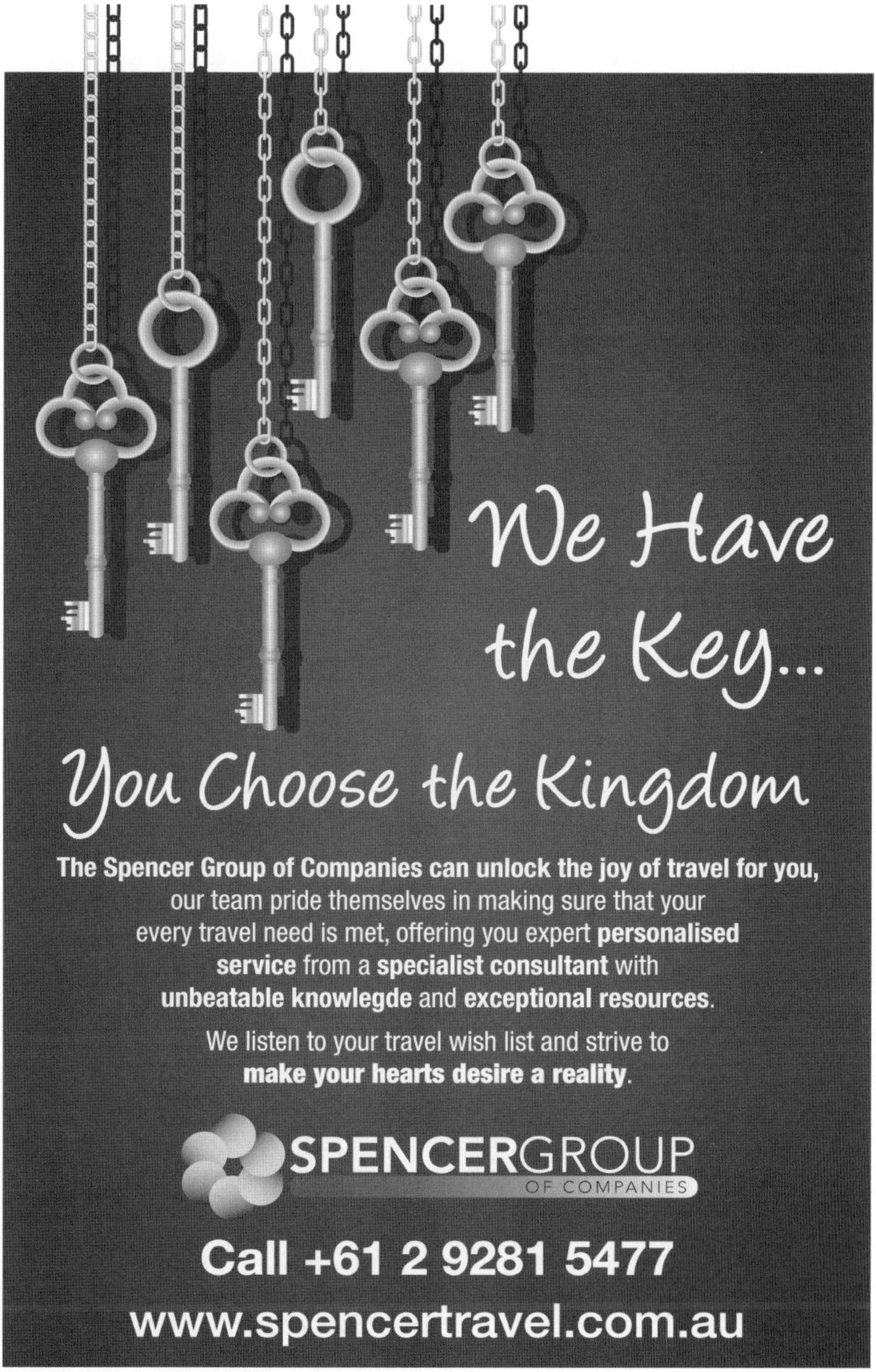